The Revival of China's Entrepreneurial Class in Historical-Comparative Perspective

The Revival of China's Entrepreneurial Class in Historical-Comparative Perspective

Michael Drake

LEXINGTON
Lanham • Boulder • New York • London

Disclaimer: All statements of fact, opinion, or analysis expressed are those of the author and do not reflect the official positions or views of the U.S. government. Nothing in the contents should be construed as asserting or implying U.S. government authentication of information or endorsement of the author's views.

Published by Lexington Books
An imprint of The Rowman & Littlefield Publishing Group, Inc.
4501 Forbes Boulevard, Suite 200, Lanham, Maryland 20706
www.rowman.com

6 Tinworth Street, London SE11 5AL, United Kingdom

British Library Cataloguing in Publication Information Available

Library of Congress Cataloging-in-Publication Data

Names: Drake, Michael, 1983- author.
Title: The revival of China's entrepreneurial class in historical-comparative perspective : prospects for a new Chinese liberalism / Michael Drake.
Description: Lanham : Lexington Books, [2020] | Includes bibliographical references and index. | Summary: "This book traces the rise, fall, and revival of China's entrepreneurial class through the lens of historical liberalism. The author argues that China's rule by law system and resultant state predation contributes to the rise of a liberal entrepreneurial class and prospects for entrepreneurial-driven political change"—Provided by publisher.
Identifiers: LCCN 2020030762 (print) | LCCN 2020030763 (ebook) | ISBN 9781793619976 (cloth) | ISBN 9781793619983 (epub)
Subjects: LCSH: Entrepreneurship—Political aspects—China. | Liberalism—China.
Classification: LCC HB615 .D695 2020 (print) | LCC HB615 (ebook) | DDC 338/.040951—dc23
LC record available at https://lccn.loc.gov/2020030762
LC ebook record available at https://lccn.loc.gov/2020030763

Contents

Acknowledgments

I am especially grateful to David for reviewing my manuscript and providing invaluable guidance throughout the course of this project. I am also deeply grateful to my very close friends—Nick, Eileen, Dan, Amy, and John—for their support, especially at very critical junctures.

Chapter One

Introduction

The Search for a Renewed Chinese Liberalism

China's political system has long been considered ideocratic in nature, that is, "a political system where the right to rule is based on the government's claim to possess special truths and insights imparted by an absolutist and comprehensive ideology" (Chang, 2002, 45–46). At certain stages in the course of China's history, this ideocratic government has held absolute power, or an ability to wield power over the development potential of economic and social structures. One consequence of this is that the possibilities for economic freedom and the rise of a modern China have been severely limited, until the decline of the Maoist state in 1978. With the advent of new economic and social structures in China, the previous absolutist-ideological frameworks—whether Confucian or socialist in nature—that acted to support an omniscient authority and passive society, have been severely compromised and de-legitimized, giving way to a degree of unrestricted space for newfound social mobilization, organization and power.

China's post-dynastic periodization can be seen as tripartite (1911–1949; 1949–1978; and post 1978), each in part characterized by attempts at socio-economic and political modernization, with varying degrees of success and catastrophe. In the initial period, China's inability to successfully modernize the nation rested in its emphasis on traditional modes of production, utilizing peasant laborers and agriculturally-based economic systems; even if commercialized, it was not mechanized and industrialized. Although localized areas of China (most emphatically the case of Shanghai) represented isolated examples of China's growing modernity, both economically and socially, overall China was unable to extend modernization from these areas to the rest of China's vast—and traditional—interior. Thus, although Chinese society in general and the elites in particular realized that China's traditional political institutions proved inadequate if not obstructive to China's development, and thus required an overhaul, the state of its social structure (peasant majority) and economic organization (commercial-agrarian) at the time of revolution ensured that a politically vacuous, underdeveloped and militarized environment would emerge in this period (Bergère, 1989; Bergère, 2009; Fairbank, 1986; Levy, 1949).

The second period, from 1949 to 1978, was a period where China had managed to find a solution to the political vacuum that had led to social and economic regression over the course of nearly four decades. Notwithstanding, though a political authority had emerged successfully claiming sole leadership over China, a different problem surfaced for China's economic growth in general, and entrepreneurial class in particular: Mao Zedong's ideological framework stipulated that all capitalist elements were enemies of the state and were subsequently liquidated from the fabric of socioeconomic life in China. Maoist socialist ideology fundamentally viewed the capitalists as class enemies and enemies of the state, where mass campaigns largely targeting the capitalists—either directly or indirectly—terrorized this class, leading to a lasting fear within their ranks (Gardner, 1969; Teiwes, 1987; Barnett, 1964).

In the third period, from 1978 until present-day, China has embarked upon a developmental path that is altogether distinct from the Republican and Maoist eras: a national political authority exists in the Chinese Communist Party (CCP), which distinguishes it from the Republican era; and entrepreneurial elements are not sought out for liquidation but instead are encouraged to produce and prosper. Nevertheless, this unprecedented shift in economic policy, and the newfound sphere of economic freedom that it has produced, has led to inevitable, and indeed (for the party) undesirable sociopolitical consequences. In short, the most significant factor behind this transformation of state and society exists within the social complexities and product of economic freedom—the emergence of a new, modern proletarian class and the possibilities for a new and rising bourgeoisie.

China's capitalist transition, and the opportunities that this newfound economic sphere presents, has facilitated the emergence of an entrepreneurial class, which has grown most significantly since the early 1990s. The private enterprise growth which occurred in the 1980s existed on a relatively small scale and consisted mostly of individual operations, while the growth beginning in the late 1980s and early 1990s, supported by favorable policy, was on a much larger scale, experiencing higher rates of entrepreneurial success, larger operations, and an increase in capital and investment (White, Howell, and Shang (WHS), 1996, 198). In 1989, only 210,000 entrepreneurs had registered; by 2007, nearly 14 million were registered (Zhang Houyi, 2004, 313; Zhang Houyi, 2006, 251; Zhang Houyi, 2007, 307; Zhang Houyi, 2009; Zhang Houyi, 1999; Zhang Houyi, 2011; Zhang Houyi, 2005, 329). Their accelerated growth in fact led to the party's unprecedented recognition, acceptance and welcoming of these new social elements into the ranks of the party organization as heard in Jiang Zemin's speech in 2001. This re-creation of the entrepreneurial class following decades of the party's assault on their existence, China's continued economic development, and now the growing antagonisms between entrepreneurs and the party surrounding legal ambiguity and state predation, have created conditions that seem increasingly favorable to the evolution of a liberal entrepreneurial class. Thus, the key political question seems to be: when will China experience the rise of a liberal entrepreneurial class both capable of, and intent on, engineering political transformation that secures the *rule of law*, direct elections, and basic freedoms that are required by this modern economic and socially complex organization? The alternative question—whether China will ever experience this political transformation—recedes with each decade.

ECONOMIC REFORMS AND THE REVIVAL OF CHINA'S ENTREPRENEURIAL CLASS

Western economic and political theory argues that the presence of opportunity through expanding markets represents the foundation for the emergence of a bourgeoisie, and that through a transforming ideology arising from its market interactions this political class would then secure political power in order to establish a democratic platform (Moore, 1966; Lipset, 1959; Lerner, 1958; Reuschemeyer, Stephens, and Stephens (RSS), 1992; Marx, 1936). Within this environment of economic development and freedom the bourgeoisie undergoes a specific (liberal) transformation—from a collection of individuals with varying interests to a class *for itself*, that is, with specific interests, and with these interests as its object. As Marx noted:

> Economic conditions had first transformed the mass of the people of the country into workers. The domination of capital has created for this mass a common situation, common interests. This mass is thus already a class as against capital, but not yet for itself. In the struggle, of which we have noted only a few phases, this mass becomes united, and constitutes itself as a class for itself. The interests it defends become class interests. But the struggle of class against class is a political struggle. . . . In the bourgeoisie we have two phases to distinguish: that in which is constituted itself as a class under the regime of feudalism and absolute monarchy, and that in which, already constituted as a class, it overthrew feudalism and monarchy to make society into a bourgeois society (Marx, 1936, 145–146).

The emergence of liberalism can be viewed through three distinct stages of social-entrepreneurial development: 1) a rationalized and secularized class, given impetus by the growth of economic freedom and independence, and demands from emerging markets, and where individual reason and thought replace adherence to traditional dogma and ideology; 2) an interest-based class, centered on the preservation of private property through the elevation of the *rule of law* and an end to the *rule by law*; and 3) a rights-based class, demanding liberal political values of political input and representation, deemed necessary for the application of a system of law founded on the belief in the intrinsic rights and value of the individual (the rule of law). Its chief consequence was the eclipsing of the traditional order, characterized by a despotic political system, an absolute guiding ideology, and a subservient social order, with those political principles distinctive of bourgeois society:

> The right to vote, representation in a legislature that makes the laws and hence is more than a rubber stamp for the executive, an objective system of law that at least in theory confers no special privileges on account of birth or inherited status, security for the rights of property and the elimination of barriers inherited from the past on its use, religious toleration, freedom of speech, and the right to peaceful assembly (Moore, 1966, 429).

The relevance of this liberal paradigm to the case of China since Reform and Opening has attracted much attention, and debate, among scholars. In the first decade of the reform era, from the end of 1978 to the end of 1989, the priority and prevailing principle was the implementation of markets and the legislation of private property in both the agricultural and industrial sectors—the same principles that had supported the rise of a Chinese bourgeoisie in the early twentieth century and that had led to a politically successful Western bourgeoisie in the eighteenth century in Europe and America. Of course and precisely because of the known connections between market expansion and social change throughout the reform period a debate was conducted between reformers, conservatives and intellectuals as to what the consequences were for China's politics in the return of markets and private property to Chinese economic development (Solinger, 1993, 225–251; Harding, 1987, 100).

The Third Plenum of the Eleventh Central Committee of the Communist Party of China in 1978 formally stated this new direction in party ideology and policy. It would reflect a new economic policy, based upon greater empowerment of the individual; enterprise efficiency and the decline of state control; greater legal institutionalization; and a political policy that would attempt to strike an end to the practice of Mao's infamous "mass line," or mass campaign and mass mobilization that formed a giant miasma over China until 1978, as well as an end to intra-party labeling (*Peking Review*, 1978, 6–16; *Renmin Ribao* (RMRB), 1979, 1). As Deng Xiaoping stated in 1978, the principles of economic organization should be "to each according his work, work out payments in accordance with the amount and quality of work done, and overcome equalitarianism; small plots of land for private use by commune members, their domestic side-occupations, and village affairs are necessary adjuncts of the socialist economy, and must not be interfered with" (Peking Review, 1978, 12). This foreshadowed a growing emphasis on privatization and the rule of law, and emerging freedoms, while moving away from the economic and social policies, including mass campaigns, that had characterized the Maoist era (Lin Chun, 2006, 207). Thus, although the party would still hold ultimate authority, this nonetheless indicated a nascent shift in power from state to society.

Discussions then ensued, some pointing out the key differences between the planned and market economies, behind the problems of the Soviet-style economic policy of centralization and unification: within this working environment, decision making rests with higher authorities, not the actual entrepreneurs; profits are distributed to the top, and enterprises aren't able to maintain equipment or improve and innovate without requests from higher governing bodies for approval and financial support. On the other hand, private enterprises and the entrepreneurs are most efficient and productive if they are empowered with individual decision making that is based on their specific conditions (Xue Muqiao, 1980, 17–18). Thus, China had slowly begun to emphasize, though not fully implement, economic freedom, market economy and private property.

Deng Xiaoping was the voice and power behind these bold new reforms in China. He not only emphasized opening China's economy to independent forces of production, but also came to promote measures to restrain official abuses through strengthening the rule of law (Deng Xiaoping, 1980). An interview with Deng Xiaoping in 1980 illuminates the shift in policy in China that commenced in 1978, and this new philosophy in support of an economic independence that Dengist pragmatism came to reflect:

> For quite a long time, we haven't had a systematic law . . . socialist democracy and a socialist legal system are not only meant to supervise the leaders and officials but also everybody has to abide by the law. At present the Chinese people are opposed to privilege. This is right . . . seek truth from facts . . . combine theory with practice and . . . proceed in every case from reality. That is to say to emancipate our mind and to think independently, but we should add another phrase to that; that is, to unite as one, look forward and march towards the four modernizations. It won't do just to obey blindly the orders from above (Deng Xiaoping, 1980, 18–19).

Upon securing leadership of the party Deng also ensured that he had liberal proponents by his side. These were to be Hu Yaobang and Zhao Ziyang, both elected to the Political Bureau in 1980, and formally announced at the Fifth Plenary Session of the Eleventh Central Committee (Peking Review, 1980b). Furthermore, at the Fifth Plenary Session he also made a formal announcement reversing the charges against Liu Shaoqi as a bourgeois proponent: “Because the appraisal of the situation in the Party and the country on the eve of the Cultural Revolution was contrary to fact, an entirely wrong and groundless inference was made, asserting that there was within the Party a counter-revolutionary revisionist line and then that there was a so-called bourgeois headquarters headed by Comrade Liu Shaoqi” (Peking Review, 1980a, 9), which followed Deng’s vindication of Peng Dehuai in his speech in 1978 at the Eleventh Central Committee (Peking Review, 1978, 14). This would set in motion a Dengist-led redemption process of those party leaders wrongfully accused during the Maoist era (Peking Review, 1980a).

These liberal economic reforms supported by a new liberal faction within the party generated a great divide among the party leadership, creating throughout the 1980s a time of constant oscillation: its pushing (liberalization of economy and society) and pulling (de-liberalization—retracting market reforms and suppressing liberal outgrowth among society) signified a relationship between Chinese state and society that was moving toward crisis. The liberal leadership welcomed market reforms and the return of the middle class, especially in its traditional role of facilitating fervent economic development, but it certainly opposed the social impact and political consequences of the growth of liberal social forces in a bourgeoisie, while the conservative faction was far more concerned about market reforms and their impact on the social and political fabric of China. The oscillations represented a political leadership attempting to circumvent the contradictions that arise in reforming economic systems without reforming political institutions (Baum, 1994, 122–142).

A speech by Deng Xiaoping, at the Second Plenary Session of the Twelfth Central Committee of the Communist Party of China, demonstrated not only his emphasis on the importance of science, technology and professionals, as well as the adoption of certain elements in Western culture, but also the contradictions that arise between the party and these social forces. Here the standard party dialogue was emphasized: reform and open to the outside world must be sought under the ideological rubric of Marxism, and defined through the leadership of the party (Deng Xiaoping, 1994, 5). Although the rise in bourgeois culture was met with party opposition, it also generated an intense effort to restructure and reform the political institutions, such as retirement mandates and changes to legislative and judicial organs. These changes served to encourage belief in political change and were reflected in the rise of the voice of intellectuals. Furthermore, although a conservative opposition rose to this development, it was soon followed by another intense reform effort by the party, this time to introduce young, educated technocrats into the party as well as the encouragement of entrepreneurial activity. The result of these profound developments would result in a mid-decade crisis for the party: the rise of corruption, as cadres increasingly became intertwined with market forces through the exploitation of state resources (Baum, 1994, 143–163).

Thus, social forces began to emerge as a result of these growing contradictions of economic reform and development, on one hand, and political rigidity on the other. This was first manifested in the Democracy Wall, where reformers encouraged the emerging liberal minds to speak freely. Although for the reformers this was a strategic move to consolidate power over the hardliners and oust Hua Guofeng, it did reflect to a certain degree the liberal nature of the reformers. Moreover, the Democracy Wall commenced a social and political trend in China: as a result of China's economic opening up, certain social elements, many former Red Guards, began to speak out and in favor of liberal principles. Participants called for the implementation of the rule of law, constitutional governance, and political pluralism in order to prevent the type of destruction and instability so characteristic of the Maoist era. Some went as far as criticizing the one-party system in general and the CCP in particular, drawing a connection between the dogmatic ideology of Marxism-Leninism and despotic governance. The crackdown on the Democracy Wall, as a result of growing criticism directed at the party and Deng Xiaoping, revealed the limits of China's constitutional governance and democratic process under the one-party system (Goldman, 1994, 41–53). As one activist stated, " 'We would like to know if it is legal or not for a vice premier and a vice chairman [Deng Xiaoping] to announce the arrest of people rather than for the courts and the people's representative organs to do so?' " (Goldman, 1994, 46). Thus, although sporadic and limited, the seeds of a Chinese liberalism had nevertheless begun to sprout.

By 1986 the liberal reformers had begun to advocate a complete withdrawal of the planned economy, where the state transitioned from its economic role as controller to regulator and facilitator. It embodied bold proposals, not only to relinquish state control, but also to implement legislation, such as developing the rule of law, in order to protect private property holders against state intrusion (Harding, 1987, 124–128). As presented at the government conference in Shanxi in 1986, members stressed the need to strengthen and perfect the "socialist legal systems" and develop "socialist democracy," specifically referring to the changing nature of the state in response to economic development (Xu Zhaoming, 1987, 28). As the term "socialist democracy" only granted a selective system of democracy to society, equally the socialist legal system granted ultimate power to the party, not an independent judiciary. Thus liberals called for the fundamentals of a democratic system: the rule of law opposed to the rule by man which guarantees that society *and* party (specifically the faction or individual in power) are accountable to the law; individual rights, such as individual freedom, political association and participation and the right of citizens to elect their officials; a system of representation, where officials are accountable to their constituency by allowing them to voice their concerns, and where freedom of the press prevails and serves its function of encouraging transparency; and finally a system of separation of powers that allows for independent government organs (Tan Jian, 1987; Wei Haibo, 1987, 74–75). The legislature should be allowed to make laws independently, as well as be able to reject proposals from the party—a concept never entertained in the history of the People's Republic of China (PRC) (Pu Xingzu, 1987, 79). As one liberal intellectual wrote:

> The power of the party committees themselves is often in the hands of a few secretaries. . . . It has seriously hindered the government, the people's representative congresses, and the judicial institutions in exercising their constitutional power. All of the top-level institutions of state power, including the government and judicial institutions, have been changed into executive organs of the party (Tan Jian, 1987, 47).

By the end of 1986, the liberal movement had reached its climax, with liberal discourse moving outside established boundaries. The effect was cumulative: discourse turned into action and demonstrations ensued. The result was a Deng Xiaoping led crackdown and the demotion of the father of liberalism in the 1980's—Hu Yaobang (Stavis, 1987). From this point through June of 1989 China would experience the death of Hu Yaobang, the rise and fall of his liberal successor Zhao Ziyang, and the Tiananmen movement followed by a severe crackdown and victory for the party, most emphatically for the conservative elements. In the aftermath of Tiananmen, it had seemed as if the possibilities for liberal political reform had permanently evaporated. Instead, in 1992 Deng Xiaoping would make his famous southern tour to advocate a return to market reforms, a move which would form the foundation for renewed and accelerated economic development.

The outcome of the Tiananmen protests in the government crackdown of social forces attempting to dialogue with the party had the effect of striking a serious blow to the hopes of those who saw a Chinese liberalism as imminent and positive for the future of China. Nonetheless, in looking back at this movement and the conditions which founded it, and the events leading up to the crackdown, it is not surprising that society had yet to acquire the power, organization and liberal tenets to effectively influence the state. The movement, which was primarily driven by students, not entrepreneurs, was unorganized, and the participants simply wanted to dialogue with the party to convey their respective frustrations related to growing corruption and inflation, among other issues produced by China's market growth amidst a lack of political reform (see Calhoun, 1997; Tsou, 1991). Indeed, at that point China was not only attempting to find the right course and speed of economic reform, all the while society was only beginning to adjust to this newfound economic environment, but moreover, the political leadership remained severely divided over economic policy as well as over how to view and handle the social product of the very reforms it had initiated.

In the wake of China's economic reforms, particularly since economic reforms accelerated in the early 1990s, discussion concerning the Western paradigm of liberal development has been renewed with much attention, resulting in differing views over the veracity of its application to China. In particular, these market reforms have given rise to possibilities for social differentiation and political agency within a new private sphere, such as that which developed and helped shape the political landscape in the course of Western development. This private associational sphere, characterized by "separation, autonomy, and voluntary association" (WHS, 1996, 11), and the diversity of interests and increasing social and economic power among its social agents, otherwise known as civil society, has struck a problematic chord when discussed in the context of China. White, Howell and Shang point to the emergence of the "market dynamic" of civil society as a result of China's reform and opening up since 1978, which reflects a transfer of power from state to society in general, and to emerging entrepreneurial elements in particular. Nevertheless, this shift in power from state to society as a result of economic freedom and growth has yet to materialize into a political force, that is, a force that dictates new rules, relationships, and institutions predicated on establishing political representation and the rule of law (WHS, 1996, 1–38). Thus, although the market dynamic—pointing to organizational activity and individual autonomy—has emerged in the reform era with greater strength than at any other point in the history of the PRC, this growing sphere nevertheless continues to contend with, and remain subordinate to, a state supervision that employs state corporatism, governs through the *rule by law*, prohibits political input, and attempts to co-opt otherwise threatening social elements (on co-optation and corporatism, see Dickson, 2008).

Indeed, the party has successfully limited the growth of this sphere while retaining its monopoly on political power. Its success in preventing the full development of a civil society at least in part can be understood in the context of China's political history and attempts at economic modernization since 1911. China's tenuous political institutions from 1911 to 1949, and the warlordism and militarization which followed, produced an enduring desire on the part of the Chinese people for a strong, predictable, and stable political authority. The destruction that wrought and wrested Chinese society, economy, and polity during the Maoist era further instilled a desire for both a political system free from internecine conflict and purges and one which can ensure economic growth and social stability. As one scholar states, "The priority given to political stability is one of the strongest and most enduring features of Chinese political culture, and seems to be shared by both state leaders and members of society. The CCP has become part of the normal order of things in China" (Dickson, 2003, 2–3). Overall the party has effectively countered both the tenuous state of political institutions during the Republican Era and the economic stasis and social upheaval that occurred under Mao.

Nevertheless, the very economic reforms that the party implemented in 1978 have not only exposed its long-standing claims to legitimacy, and in turn caused people to reconsider its ability to effectively govern, but they have also created social elements which are questioning the veracity of the party's monopoly on political power. Since traditional claims to political legitimacy—Confucian-based claims to morality or revolutionary ideals and goals—have eroded, the party has had to develop new forms of legitimacy, particularly the current claim to its indispensable position in guiding and developing China's economic transition. As Hu Jintao stated in his speech at the 90th anniversary of the CCP: "Looking back at China's development and progress over the past 90 years, we have naturally come to this basic conclusion: Success in China hinges on the Party" (Beijing Review, 2011). Thus, the party has attempted to leverage its command over China's economic development as a way to legitimize its monopoly on political power. These party-led reforms have become a double-edge sword: on one hand they have blessed the party by creating newfound and unprecedented prosperity for the people, some of whom in turn view the party favorably; on the other hand, they have created new—disenfranchised and disaffected—social elements which threaten the party's continued hold on political power.

In light of these conditions, and with the erosion of this cultural and ideological glue, which traditionally has upheld the party as the vanguard political authority, it has increasingly relied upon methods which seek to control and divert potentially autonomous social forces, and thus sustain a Leninist regime overseeing capitalist transition. In particular, the party has employed the methods of co-optation and corporatism, which in general, seek to prevent the formation of a civil society, and in particular, the development of new, independent, and politically conscious social agents, organized in a way that could threaten the party's monopoly on political power. The party's emphasis on these very methods reveal that economic growth alone may not be enough to distract or align otherwise autonomous and politicized social forces, while quite possibly even signaling the emergence of social agents, which as a result of China's economic reforms, demand substantive legal and political reform.

As a result, since China opened its doors to the outside world in 1978, a heated discussion has ensued related to the social outcomes and political consequences of its economic transition, particularly, whether or not new liberal social elements (particularly entrepreneurs) have emerged paralleling the social forces that evolved in the course of Western democratic development. Some scholars have concluded that a liberal (and thus potentially politically active and party-opposed) entrepreneurial class remains largely absent in contemporary China (see Dickson, 2008, 2010; Tsai, 2007). Firstly, some point to the party's recruitment of entrepreneurs and the observed symbiosis between them, otherwise known as the party's mechanism of co-optation (Dickson, 2008). State co-optation—mediated by party membership—has been introduced in order to compensate for the erosion of traditional political institutions which, absent the current sphere of economic freedom and growth, had previously represented the most viable path to a position of prosperity and power. Jiang Zemin's speech in 2001 officially welcomed China's private entrepreneurs into the party. As China's former leader stated:

> There are, among others, entrepreneurs and technical personnel employed by scientific and technical enterprises of the non-public sector, managerial and technical staff employed by foreign-funded enterprises, the self-employed, private entrepreneurs, employees in intermediaries and free-lance professionals. . . . Under the guidance of the Party's line, principles and policies, most of these people in the new social strata have contributed to the development of productive forces and other undertakings in a socialist society through honest labor and work or lawful business operation. . . . The basic components and backbone of the Party are those from workers, farmers, intellectuals, servicemen and cadres. At the same time, it is also necessary to accept those outstanding elements from other sectors of the society who have subscribed to the Party's program and Constitution, worked for the Party's line and program wholeheartedly, and proved to meet the requirements for the Party membership through a long period of tests (Jiang Zemin, 2001, v).

Jiang Zemin's announcement was profound in that the party had explicitly sanctioned a class—"honest" and "outstanding elements"—that historically had been demonized, ostracized and eventually liquidated by the party; thus, this proclamation reveals just how imperative this class is to the party's future. Under this arrangement, the state benefits by a) absorbing autonomous and powerful social agents that otherwise could act against the interests of the party; and b) by leveraging their skills and resources necessary to fuel economic modernization, which is crucial to ensuring the party's continued legitimacy (Dickson, 2008, 66–100). In return, entrepreneurs enjoy a host of privileges. As Dickson notes: "Party membership gives entrepreneurs easier access to loans, official discretion in granting licenses and permits. . . . Party membership not only provides discernible benefits but may also allow entrepreneurs to avoid the interference of party and government organizations in their business affairs" (ibid, 94). This observed symbiosis in contemporary China is reminiscent of the dynastic relationship between the state and the individual, mediated by the civil service examination, whereby the state absorbed otherwise powerful and autonomous social agents and leveraged their skills and resources to its advantage; in return, civil servants enjoyed an array of economic, legal, and social benefits (see chapter 3 for more details on this topic).

Secondly, the state employs a corporatist model to influence and control China's emerging entrepreneurial class (Dickson, 2008, 101–135). Corporatism, like co-optation, has emerged as an important strategy for counteracting the party's weakening grip on (potentially autonomous and powerful) social and economic forces produced by the very market reforms and economic freedom it initiated in 1978. Whereas co-optation essentially seeks to lure social agents into the party machine, corporatism seeks to control those outside of the party apparatus, analogous to the "mass organizations" of the Maoist years (Dickson, 2008, 110). Corporatism is a system in which the state licenses an umbrella organization to represent the interests of a particular social group. In this way the state indirectly controls the organization and proliferation of interests and groups by influencing leadership and activities, while in effect also preventing other organizations from representing particular interests. Termed "incorporation" by some scholars, this state-centered corporatism "has been a force for co-optation and control . . . [and] has also operated as a screening device to exclude organizations seen as unnecessary, unacceptable or threatening" (White, Howell and Shang, 1996, 33; see also Dickson, 2008, 101–135).

In the case of private entrepreneurs and private enterprises, three organizations act as the official business associations through which the party exercises oversight and control of their activities: the Private Enterprises Associations, the Self-Employed Laborers Association, and the Industrial and Commercial Federation. These associations facilitate links between businesses and the party and help the party watch and direct their activities. (Dickson, 2008, 101–135).

Other scholars, on the other hand, see emerging conditions favorable to the evolution of liberal social agents: an emergence of a new generation without reference to China's Maoist and revolutionary traditions; the emergence of "netizens" and micro-blogs which now command millions of users, reflecting a new and powerful vehicle for mobilization and self-expression; pervasive corruption, increasingly visible to Chinese society as the income gap continues to widen, especially among entrepreneurs (Liu and Chen, 2012); the rise of new spheres of power outside the state as the private sector grows and the party struggles to maintain its political power and social controls (WHS, 1996, 203–207); protests spearheaded by the middle class and organized through the Internet (Cheng Li, 2010, 75); and the emergence of the *Baling Hou* generation of entrepreneurs. Indeed, a particular concern for the CCP is that China's market reforms have revived the entrepreneurial class and provided them with new opportunities for wealth, power and organization independent of the party (WHS, 1996, 13). As Cheng Li notes "They [Chinese scholars] argue that one should rethink the possible political role of the middle class in this rapidly changing country. Just as yesterday's political target could be today's political ally, so could today's political ally become tomorrow's political rabble-rouser" (Cheng Li, 2010, 72).

Yet other scholars have highlighted how Xi Jinping's China is reasserting the party's control over society and economy, including Internet controls and prioritizing SOE's over private enterprise (Economy, 2018; Lardy, 2019). Although China has supervised and regulated Internet activity for decades, Xi Jinping has expanded China's Internet controls in recent years, calling into question the extent to which netizens can express their opinions, and organize to advance their interests, online. According to Elizabeth Economy, China began developing a supervisory apparatus to control the Internet well before Xi's rise to power, which included creating a firewall, implementing new regulations, and employing a cyber army to influence and control online discussion. Yet, netizens were increasingly afforded the space online to expose official corruption and unfair treatment of individuals, especially toward the end of Hu Jintao's reign. However, the former optimism among netizens under the reign of Hu Jintao, particularly concerning the ability to leverage the Internet to organize around particular interests and expose corruption, has, to some degree, reversed course under Xi Jinping. Xi has made it a point to resume greater control over the online world by assuming a more direct line of control over the bureaucracies that supervise Internet behavior, developing new Internet supervision technology, and adding laws to criminalize behavior (Economy, 2018, 55–90).

To be sure, social unrest and protests, including those organized through the Internet, have not ended under Xi. Indeed, these have continued, and are further detailed in chapter 7. Furthermore, this drive to suppress Internet freedom comes at a cost to the party, particularly an economic cost (Economy,

2018, 55–90). In turn, it threatens to upend the party's primary source of legitimacy—economic growth—and add to private entrepreneurs' already long list of grievances—grievances that have the potential to develop into demands for legal and political reforms.

Xi has also decided to re-prioritize China's state-owned enterprises (SOEs) following years of reform (Economy, 2018, 104–105; Lardy, 2019, 16–17). The logic behind this appears to be threefold: to limit unemployment and thereby limit social unrest and protest; to leverage SOEs in support of China's Belt and Road Initiative (BRI); and to appease SOE officials who prefer to retain their lucrative positions (Economy, 2018, 108–110; Lardy, 2019, 122–125)). However, this has come at considerable economic cost. SOEs continue to be grossly inefficient and experience significant financial losses, and the continuation of this policy threatens to derail China's economic growth (Lardy, 2019). This, in turn, also threatens to erode the party's last and most prominent source of legitimacy: its claim to be the source of China's high-speed economic growth. Indeed, the party itself, even under Xi Jinping, appears to continue to acknowledge the necessity of the private sector, evidenced in the unprecedented language produced during the Third Plenum of the 18th Chinese Communist Party Congress explicating the importance of the market economy, as well as in its recent push to prioritize the private sector:

> President Xi Jinping in late September [2018] publicly emphasized the importance of private firms to the success of the Chinese economy. The following month Liu He chaired a meeting of China's top financial regulatory body that endorsed specific measures for easing financial difficulties of private firms. Early the following month central bank governor Yi Gang announced a series of new policies to increase bank loans and bond and equity financing for private firms. A few days later Guo Shuqing, the head of China's bank and insurance regulator, put forth a specific target that no less than 50 percent of new corporate loans should go to private companies over the next three years (Lardy, 2019, 111–112).

Ultimately, the critical importance of the private sector for the continued growth of China's economy—and the party's legitimacy—and the resultant expansion of the entrepreneurial class over the past thirty years without requisite legal reforms, the rise of the *Baling Hou* generation of entrepreneurs, the availability—if not proliferating use—of technology and Internet mediums to organize, associate, and project one's voice, especially among entrepreneurs, and questions concerning the degree to which these young entrepreneurs are motivated to wed with the party, begs the question: to what extent are these social agents developing along a liberal trajectory in the economic, legal, and political sense of the term? In remaining consistent with the historical trajectory of liberal development (classical liberalism), the widespread expression of economic freedom in China, set against a lack of legal institutionalization, should foster the rise of a new—and liberal—entrepreneurial class. In particular, the author hypothesizes that this will produce an entrepreneurial class which has the potential to become a bourgeoisie, that is, a capital-owning class *for itself* with property-law interests: a class demanding the *rule of law* (founded on the belief in the intrinsic rights and value of the individual) over the *rule by law* (founded on the belief that the party and its interests are paramount, and supersede the rights of the individual), and political input and representation in order to check state predation and protect private property. Therefore, the possibility for a new and liberal Chinese entrepreneurial class, a class *for itself*, deserves particular scholarly attention.

ORGANIZATION OF RESEARCH AND FINDINGS

This volume seeks to analyze the variables which determined the evolution of political liberalism in the West, to construct a model of these relationships, and to employ this model to understand the extent to which China is experiencing a similar trajectory, including whether or not China's emerging entrepreneurial class is evolving along liberal (economic, legal and political) lines. In turn, the author hopes to uncover new insights into an emerging and relatively unknown social class in contemporary China, and from this to understand if the possibility exists for a new Chinese liberalism.

In examining China's entrepreneurial class, the author employed textual analysis of Chinese-language materials, including social surveys, economic data and interviews with entrepreneurs, and conducted in-depth personal interviews with Chinese entrepreneurs from 2010–2012. The entrepreneurs the author interviewed were based in either Beijing or Shanghai and managed small to medium size enterprises; their ages ranged from 27–50, though the vast majority fell between 27–37 years old. They represented a wide range of industries: construction, mobile application development, restaurant, consulting, tourism, entertainment, advertising, business incubator, food import, advertising, real estate, graphic design, and online food service.

The interviews focused on three areas of the entrepreneur's life: China's market reforms and growing wealth, particularly, are they rational and autonomous economic actors and thinkers?; the property-law environment, including the issue of official graft in China, particularly—do they perceive a need for the rule *of* law over the rule *by* law?; and the political life of the entrepreneur, particularly—are they forming liberal political values? The author focused primarily on what has been coined the *Baling Hou* generation of entrepreneurs, technically those born after 1980, though the author included in this category those born as early as the mid-1970s. This particular group of entrepreneurs is significant in that they are emerging post-revolution, with no direct experience of the economic, social and political characteristics of the Maoist era. Instead, they are absent the traditional mold that many entrepreneurs have carried with them into the reform era and which previously had facilitated an entrepreneurial evolution along conservative lines. Moreover, relatively little is known about this generation of entrepreneurs. Interviews were thus effective in not only gaining insight into these social elements but also in an effort to avoid limited or incomplete responses.

Chapter 2 explores the following question: what were the variables that guided the Western historical evolution of an entrepreneurial class and that produced a liberal ruling class: a bourgeoisie? The chapter examines the independent variables that surrounded the Western historical evolution of the liberal entrepreneurial class in the transition from a feudal-agrarian and absolutist system to a modern-capitalist and democratic nation, including how they interacted and evolved to produce a liberal ruling class. The type of economic organization that prevailed, the growth of land and labor markets, the strength and expansion of markets, lack of legal protections, particularly pertaining to private property and a free and predictable economic sphere, and emerging business, capitalist, and entrepreneurial elements increasingly independent of the state, all influenced the evolution—and indeed the full maturation—of a liberal entrepreneurial class. The consequence was substantive political institutional change. Although England and France experienced similar political transformations, their respective paths proved distinct due to differences in the traditional socioeconomic and political environments, and how they interacted.

Chapter 3 explores the following questions: why was the full maturation of a liberal entrepreneurial class halted in both Imperial China and the Republican era?; and why did the PRC crush the business class and with what kinds of social and political consequences? The chapter traces China's unique development from the Song dynasty through the first thirty years of the PRC. It begins by examining China's limited economic development, in both the dynastic and Republican periods, and its social and political outcome, before turning to the near liquidation of China's entrepreneurs under Mao. To be sure, China experienced technological innovation and economic growth centuries before that of England in particular, and Europe in general, most notably during the Song dynasty (960–1279), beginning in the tenth century. Nonetheless, overall, China's economic development remained limited to commercialization, while utilizing traditional relations of production, increasingly relying on its accelerating population growth, and emphasizing an agrarian order, the reasons for which will be detailed in this chapter. As a consequence, the evolution of a liberal entrepreneurial class remained limited to its first phase of development—that of a rational entrepreneurial class. The result was the rise of conservative social forces in opposition to the Qing regime, which overthrew the dynasty in 1911 and signaled a permanent end to Imperial China.

The Republican period, specifically from 1911–1937, was a politically oscillating period for China at best and a politically vacuous period at worst—a condition which ultimately limited the otherwise unprecedented development of China's social organization and economic sphere. Shanghai exemplified the localized socioeconomic development at that time, especially by the 1920s: a thriving epicenter of economic exchange and native industrial growth; a social organization of growing complexity and rising entrepreneurship; and a resultant social class formation that was increasingly imbued with bourgeois characteristics. But the grave lack of economic development in late dynastic China created deleterious conditions for post-revolution China: an underdeveloped liberal society and the continuation of a conservative elite, which degenerated into a period of provincialism, warlordism, and civil war.

Following the Sino-Japanese War and the Chinese Civil War (between the CCP and Kuomintang (KMT)), the CCP emerged as the political victor, consolidated its power and authority over China, and established itself as the one and only legitimate party and governor of China. Although the initial years of the party's political control seemed to accept the capitalist class as part of China's social organization, the party's acceptance of their existence was out of necessity for the consolidation of its power. Once Mao believed the party had established its base, a reign of terror began, directed at any and all social elements considered to be "bourgeoisie." This manifested in the ensuing Five-Anti Campaign, and the numerous campaigns that followed targeting other specific groups such as intellectuals, and eventually the entire order, witnessed in the Great Leap Forward and the Great Proletarian Cultural Revolution (GPCR). Deng Xiaoping, who personally witnessed the events of the Maoist period and who was indeed a victim himself at times, was resolved to find a solution. The decision to reform and open up in 1978 forged a breach in the former ideological and organizational framework, which has led to the growth of liberal social forces.

Chapter 4 explores the following questions: why did the PRC purposefully re-invent the entrepreneurial class and with what kinds of social and political consequences?; and to what extent are China's entrepreneurs becoming rational economic actors and autonomous thinkers? The chapter examines the degree to which Chinese entrepreneurs are exercising economic rationality, autonomy and ideological detachment from the party. The mid-1990s marked a historic development in the history of China's socioeconomic development, specifically the accelerated growth of a private economic sphere and the subsequent growth of its social product in the rise of the private entrepreneur and private enterprise. Historically, this growth marked the growing independence of the entrepreneur—that in conjunction with interactions with market mechanisms—became increasingly rational. As a consequence, the entrepreneur became progressively detached from a blind indifference and subservience to the state and more concerned about economic life, the economic environment, and personal freedoms. To be sure, the party has attempted to preempt this development, by adapting its ideological foundation from Confucianism and socialism and towards a modern nationalism, which begs the question—to what extent are Chinese entrepreneurs becoming liberal in the economic sense of the term?

Chapter 5 explores the following questions: what is the nature of corruption in contemporary China?; To what extent has China's embrace of the *rule by law* exacerbated corruption and state predation, particularly as it affects the entrepreneurial class?; and are China's entrepreneurs forming and advancing legal and property-law interests as a result of China's rule by law environment? Within China there is a growing contention between China's entrepreneurial class and their evolving property-law interests on one hand, and a gross lack of legal institutionalization and pervasive state predation on the other. Although the party has revised the constitution to make concessions towards the entrepreneurs and their growing imperative for property protection, these measures have remained artificial, and will continue to remain so as long as China's one-party closed political system remains. As a consequence of the absence of effective measures to ensure property protection, and with the rise of state predation manifested in the rise of bribery, extortion, profiteering, arrogation of private property, and abuse of policing powers, entrepreneurs are beginning to form an interest in creating a predictable environment of economic freedom and legal protection within which they can conduct their economic activities.

Chapter 6 explores the following question: to what extent does China's entrepreneurial class embody liberal political characteristics, such as independence from the party, political awareness, and political agency, including active engagement in political discussion and organization? As a result of not only the growth of economic freedom and ideological independence, but also the growth of property-law interests, an entrepreneurial class has begun to ascend and form into a class for itself some evidence suggests—with liberal economic, legal, and political interests as its object. The entrepreneurial class has indicated a shift in its political alignment, that is, a break from dependence on political institutions and growing sense of independence. Furthermore, the entrepreneurial class has indicated signs of a growing political awareness as well as an emphasis on political values such as the separation of powers and fundamental rights and freedoms, which reflect the growth of liberal values. Finally, the emergence of the *Baling Hou* generation, in particular, reflects the potential for a renewed growth of liberal forces. This generation appears to be especially independent-minded and innovative, regularly uses Internet mediums as vehicles for discussion and organization, and lacks personal experience in, or association with, pre-reform China. Thus, they pose a new potential threat to the CCP, its monopoly on political power, and its quest for continued legitimacy, and appear to understand the inadequacies of China's one-party system. Will these emergent social agents further buttress the party and its grip on political power, or will they organize in pursuit of their (historically) most cherished interests: the rule of law and political representation?

Chapter Two

Liberal Class Development in England and France

For most of history, economic activity remained limited and isolated, and land and labor were regulated through feudal organization and gild system. Thus society remained unchanged. Economic crises and opportunities, which emerged as social classes battled for their respective interests, in Western Europe eventually led to incentives to produce for expanding markets, incentives which provided the catalyst for the rise of machines and the Industrial Revolution. Previous economy activity, which had remained an outgrowth of traditional society, was displaced by the emergence of the market economy, which meant absorbing land and labor into the economic organism of exchange. This new form of economic organization had the effect of slowly displacing the power of the state with that of society and thereby eroding state power, while transforming the fabric of society. This paved the way for political institutional change, particularly the birth of democratic institutions in Western Europe (Polanyi, 1957, 68–76).

The consequence of this newfound economic sphere was the emergence of a new social class structure, one not only increasingly stratified, but one that heralded a novel entrepreneurial class—innovating in ways, and producing on a scale, never seen before. Both England and France provide key examples of this nexus between capitalist development and expanding economic freedoms, social class evolution and the rise of liberal elements, and political change. England's development reveals the nature of the impact to the social structure when a profusion of incentives exist to produce along capitalist lines, while encountering an increasingly predatory state apparatus. France on the other hand, demonstrates how incentives, or lack thereof, can temporarily work in the opposite direction—creating and wedding conservative elements against the state and impeding the growth of an (liberal) entrepreneurial class. This chapter seeks to illuminate the particular variables in England and

France which led to the creation of an entrepreneurial class, particularly a liberal entrepreneurial class.

SOCIOPOLITICAL TRANSFORMATION IN ENGLAND: THE GRADUAL ROUTE TO LIBERAL VALUES AND INSTITUTIONS

The changing landscape in England, beginning as early as the thirteenth century, was one in which social disruption, dislocation, and cleavage, in conjunction with market opportunities and market forces, fueled an unprecedented economic growth and with it the transformation of England's social structure, the consequence of which was political institutional change—that is, democracy (Moore, 1966; Brenner, 1985; Macfarlane, 1978). As Moore explains, social actors of the revolutions, produced from the throes of economic transformation, decided the political organization of the state, where specific corollaries can be seen between peasant revolution and communism, a state-bourgeoisie coalition (top-down revolution) and fascism, and bourgeois revolution and democracy. The most decisive factor was relative class power within the social structure, in particular, to what extent the peasant class was reduced and to what extent the nobility and landed elite were assimilated into the ranks of the bourgeoisie. Democracy succeeded in societies where the process of economic growth and subsequent social structural changes became increasingly composed of liberal social elements who demonstrated autonomy from the ruler, commanded a powerful socioeconomic base, and assimilated other—and otherwise powerful and conservative—social elements. Ultimately, social revolution or civil war was the culmination of the contradictions between a bourgeois society and traditional political institutions. As Moore notes,

> Revolutionary violence and/or civil war prepared the way for liberalism, and later democracy, in the three main centers where these institutions first grew up: England, France, and the United States. This violence severely weakened institutions and social groups opposed to these trends. After the execution of Charles I no English King tried to rule without Parliament. The French Revolution dealt a crippling blow to the monarchy and aristocracy. In the United States the American Revolution put an end to what limited possibility there may have been for foreign domination. American social and political questions could not be decided in London (Moore, 1989, 10).

England's socioeconomic structure prior to the thirteenth century followed that of the traditional feudal order. Within feudal organization peasant families or clans served as the traditional unit of ownership, production and consumption, producing primarily for consumption and operating in isolation of markets, while remaining immobile. The peasant communities were organized under the village, all of which existed within a particular lord's domain, specifically the manor, through which the lord exercised immense jurisdictional power over subordinate social elements. Customs, which were determined by the courts, did theoretically provide legal protection to unfree tenants (villeins), but the reality was that lords used their political power to control the courts, and in doing so were able to wield considerable power over the economic activities of tenants (Martin, 1983, 36–37). This legal and political power provided the basis for the lord's extraction of economic surplus: any excess production was allocated to the lords and the state for the cost of maintaining the lifestyles of the aristocratic families and for maintaining a military, but these surpluses were rarely used for investment which could influence economic productivity and expansion (Hilton, 1985). Despite its persistence for centuries, this feudal organism began to break down in England as early as the thirteenth and fourteenth centuries, where previously entrenched social customs and economic activities—collective customs of labor and ownership—were slowly replaced by emphasis on the individual, private property and economic efficiency and productivity (Macfarlane, 1978).

The nature of the lords' revenue marked the catalyst for the commencement of England's long and gradual socioeconomic transformation. So long as lords maintained satisfactory revenues through surplus extraction, and as long as peasants remained on the land, producing for subsistence and without surplus to invest in greater productivity, the traditional feudal order remained intact. However, in England, the early and gradual development which followed the dislocation of the feudal order derived not only from a fundamental and growing problem within the feudal structure—the precariousness if not decline of the feudal lord's income—as it also did in France, but more importantly, from how the landowning classes responded to this crisis. In other words, this crisis was in part the product of successful peasant organization and revolt in England and France (also influenced by plague, lordly competition and the ultimate inefficiency of the feudal mode of production), an activity which did not predominate among the peasantry of eastern Europe. Thus feudal lords, who had typically derived their incomes from squeezing peasants, acquiring new lands or extracting land or labor from other lords, were forced to find alternative methods. The French nobility, in response to this situation, were afforded the strength of the absolutist state, which temporarily assumed the political power they had lost over the peasantry; the English landowning classes had no such recourse (Brenner, 1985; 1985b, 226).

The eventual decline in income forced these landowning agents to find and adopt other methods, which in England had the effect of dissolving serfdom and replacing it with capitalist activity and productivity in the countryside (Hilton, 1985). As Brenner notes, English "lords were obliged to use their remaining feudal powers to further what in the end turned out to be capitalist development" (1985b, 293). They did not, as their counterparts did in France, use their capital to invest in privileges and immunities granted by the state (the sale of offices). The English state, due to its lack of strength and available resources, simply could not attract these social elements; thus incentives in England led to a very different socioeconomic trajectory—one where individual advancement was achieved through economic investment and greater economic productivity (Martin, 1983, 103).

The evolution of Common Law and then the 1381 Peasants' Revolt provided the first blow to England's traditional feudal structure and the revenue dilemmas faced by lords, which was then accelerated by the plague and the economic crisis that followed. As of 1200, the majority of tenants operated within the "unfree" category, though within a century the development of rights afforded by Common Law created a degree of separation between peasants and lords. Then came the plague in 1349, from which at least half of the population perished, causing economic catastrophe along the way: crops and livestock were abandoned, and famines ensued resulting in a crisis of labor. As a result, the nature of land and labor, which for centuries had persisted according to the dictates of feudalism, was transformed: statutory labor ceased to exist, and land became commoditized (Tombs, 2014, 87–125).

The process of agricultural transformation, in the fourteenth and fifteenth centuries, began with the move toward advancements in the techniques of husbandry, which had remained focused on arable land and its cultivation. Peasants became "more vigorous and enterprising," and in turn, began opposing the prevailing framework of communal land and servitude while pressing for greater independence and individual land (Lipson, 1920, 120–125). Instead of suppressing this activity by extracting all production from the peasantry, and thereby encouraging the continuation of the feudal mode of production and feudal relations, landlords embraced agrarian capitalism and began breaking away from the feudal institutions and relationships which had persisted for centuries. Thus, the rise of capitalist relations in the countryside during this period provided fuel behind England's economic advance and social class transformation (Croot and Parker, 1985). As a result, the system of large estates and agrarian elite commanding a mass of laborers on the land with limited opportunity for mobilization or land acquisition began to break down, which was gradually replaced by economic efficiency, investment, and production for the market. As Martin points out: "The introduction of rotating arable and ley pastures, or up-and-down husbandry; the floating of water meadows; new fallow crops and selected grasses; marsh drainage; fertilizers and stock-breeding—all required considerable investment of capital and revolutionized the productivity of land, doubling or tripling it" (1983, 132).

The displacement and elimination of peasants in order to maximize production and profit, or the enclosure movement, defined by Martin as "the extinction of common rights, depopulation, engrossing and conversion" (1983, 132)), accelerated economic and social transformation. The enclosure movement, which separated peasants from their means of subsistence (their land, tools, etc.), transformed the relations of production, which coupled with a rising capitalist class in the countryside, formed the foundation for the unprecedented economic development that would follow in England (Brenner, 1985b). In the case of unenclosed peasant farms, such as existed in many other parts of Europe, although higher yields were possible, they were generated through added labor inputs and intensification instead of through labor-saving methods—such as investments in farm equipment and adoption of new methods of production. Even in the case of France, where large farms existed, their functions were entirely different than those in England—labor-intensive methods through peasant production prevailed over labor-saving methods. The result was the stunting of economic development in many parts of Europe, while England's development gradually advanced (Moore, 1966, 3–39; Tawney, 1912, 55–97; Brenner, 1985b).

Rational enterprising elements, primarily drawn from the enclosing agents, the gentry and yeoman, began to emerge in the economic sense of the term, that is, using land to produce for markets, and for profit, making investments, and capitalizing on opportunities in growing markets (Martin, 1983, 137–138; Moore, 1966, 4). As Martin writes, "there was a shift from large landlords towards the gentry and capitalist farmers and lessees as the dominant enclosing group" (Martin, 1983, 137–138). As a consequence, this economic activity and growth vitiated feudal organization and diminished the ideological power of the church and absolutist state. In turn it created new social elements, with new ideas of organization, that were becoming increasingly rational, in an economic sense, and autonomous, or detached from the ideological controls of the church and state (Moore, 1966, 4–5). These social elements realized the potential for profits through growing markets for wool, and began re-purposing land to produce for these markets, whether directly or by leasing their lands; and merchants in the cities equally recognized this opportunity investing in land in an effort to enter the wool industry (Moore, 1966, 9; Lipson, 1920, 115–195; Martin, 1983, 132–138). Thus, the fundamental utility of land had changed from cultivation for subsistence to production for profit (Tawney, 1912, 6). As Marx writes:

> This industry opened new outlets for wool. In order to produce wool on a large scale, arable land had to be transformed into pasturage. To effect this transformation, the estates had to be concentrated. To concentrate the estates, small holdings had first to be abolished, thousands of tenants had to be driven from their native soil and a few shepherds in charge of millions of sheep to be installed in their place. Thus, by successive transformations, landed property in Scotland has resulted in the driving out of men by sheep (1936, 101).

The growth of the wool trade initially provided the strongest motivation for the enclosure movement, which facilitated capitalist development and social-structural transformation, while distant markets for cloth also further stimulated this economic transformation. For one, sheep rearing and wool cultivation became especially attractive in those regions where clay predominated, as this soil base was more advantageous to grass than arable farming. In addition to this, wool drew relatively high profits due to its light weight and convenience of transport, as well as its profit advantage over grain markets (Moore, 1966, 3–39). Furthermore, and directly related to the incentive to enclose, "sheep-grazing . . . required an absolute minimum of 50 acres of pasture and a large outlay on stock, rent, and feed for its profitable operation" (Martin, 1983, 133).

Further, at the very time when the cloth markets, which had prospered not only in England but throughout many parts of Europe, faced contraction, England, due to the very capitalist shift it had begun to embrace and the rising purchasing power among individuals which sprung from this shift, experienced a substantive growth in domestic markets and thus the move from exporting to importing products. This included the importation of silk to be used in the production of cheap items for middle and low-income classes, as well as a number of food products, including raisins, tobacco, and sugar. As the price of agricultural products dropped, and purchasing power increased, demands grew for non-agricultural consumer products, which fueled the growth of new industries. As a result of this economic transformation, the social structure also transformed, producing a middle class in general and a rising stratum of capitalist-entrepreneurs, in the cities, in particular (Brenner, 1993, 40–44).

These aforementioned conditions and incentives culled individuals further toward capitalist logic. Former feudal conditions, whereby peasants held and cultivated land which provided their means of subsistence, and who were under the control of lords including the appropriation of surpluses, transformed into capitalist conditions whereby peasants either became tenant-farmers or displaced laborers, and whereby markets and competition dictated production. The abolition of feudal-lordly controls over farmers, and their power to extract and appropriate as a form of revenue, was replaced by tenants' rents. This then had the effect of forcing farmers to calculate production beyond subsistence, and to produce within a competitive environment and for growing markets in order to maintain their position on the land, which in turn, motivated farmers to both specialize and effectually produce. As a consequence, those unable to effectively compete were displaced by efficient capitalist farmers, while producing the positive effect of increasing the purchasing power of individuals (Brenner, 1993; Brenner, 1985b, 296–297).

Furthermore, by the end of the sixteenth century and after massive military campaigns that decimated the Crown's coffers and forced it to sell off most of its lands to the landed classes, due to a declining need to devote time and resources to military preparedness, the English noble classes shed what had been part and parcel to their existence—military prowess—and replaced it with economic pursuits, particularly those related to the wool trade, among other growing industries (Anderson, 2013, 125–126). In other words they no longer relied upon the political backing of the Crown to sanction feudal relations and their ability to impose "extra-economic compulsion" in order to generate revenue. Instead, they had found an alternate source of revenue without the Crown in the equation, and were increasingly content with the income obtained through the emerging land and labor markets (Brenner, 1993, 204). To the extent that they did retain their military proclivities, through a growing and eventually superior naval force and fleet, it was equally if not soon predominantly purposed for trade, which further acted to fuse commercial and landed class elements (Anderson, 2013, 134–135).

Within this socioeconomic backdrop, a fundamental contradiction began to surface. The political-legal institutions of feudalism, which for a time had provided lords with immense jurisdictional power, had by this time severely disintegrated. As these institutions eroded, English absolutism attempted to fill its place (Anderson, 2013, 19; Martin, 1983). Indeed, at the turn of the sixteenth century the political situation had become increasingly dictated by the economic changes that were sweeping throughout the country: on one hand lords could no longer coercively marshal subjects into war, while on the other hand the crown held little direct control over a military force (Tombs, 2014, 195–196). Absolutism depended upon the continuation of feudal relations of production, particularly the continuation of the peasantry as the primary source of revenue, which became increasingly threatened by the growth of economic opportunity and the shift toward agrarian capitalism and capitalist relations of production. Thus, as time pressed on, the interests of the landed classes (to which the Crown needed to attend) increasingly conflicted with the interests of the state: capitalist activity—particularly enclosure—invariably eliminated the peasantry, and severed dependence on, and any allegiance to, the Crown. The result was that the Crown had to find new sources of revenue in order to fund its avarice, provide public services and goods, and arguably most of all, to fund defense and military campaigns, which it found through the taxation of a growing commercial and industrial sphere—the consequence of which was to eventually induce powerful opposition from below (Brenner, 1993).

As mentioned above, England's capitalist-agrarian transformation created a new enterprising social class and eventually a new urban middle class. The rise of this entrepreneurial class can be traced back to the formation of the merchant corporations, which were blessed by the Crown with exclusive rights to trade. In return, the Crown received much needed revenues in the form of taxation from the merchants or even in loans, as well as their allegiance (Brenner, 1993, 200). The established corporations ("government-chartered monopoly corporation" (Brenner, 1993, 85), sanctioned by the Crown and lobbied for by the Merchants) effectively restricted access to expanding markets and limited the number of merchants that could join merchant corporations. In regard to limited merchant membership, artisans and shopkeepers, or small and direct producers, were the primary targets of the Merchants' corporation, since by excluding these particular groups from membership and monopolizing the trade they prevented a direct relationship between the producer and buyer, and thereby controlled prices and profit margins. For the Merchants Adventurers it was preventing cloth producers from trading around the merchants; and for the Levant Merchants it was preventing domestic retailers and producers in the import business from circumventing the merchant intermediary and thereby threatening their profits (Brenner, 1993, 83–85): "The result was naturally a significant hardening of the lines that already divided the company merchants from the rest of the City's business community, and an increase in the potential for open hostilities between the two" (Brenner, 1993, 84).

The social consequences of England's government-sanctioned merchant syndicates, which excluded those individuals that had neither the wealth nor political connections to enter these companies and benefit from their trade, was to propel the excluded "domestic shopkeepers, ship captain and domestic traders" to engage the more speculative and precarious colonial crop production and trade, and through this to produce the need for "innovation and diversification" (Brenner, 1993, 159–160). Representing the seeds for the coming conflict between these capitalist entrepreneurs and the Crown's usurpations—including prohibitive taxation and arrogation of property—were these very economic opportunities developing in America, particularly the tobacco and sugar trades. Although the powerful London merchant corporations, and wealthy gentry, initially considered engaging in economic opportunities in the American colonies, they quickly dropped the idea since neither merchants nor gentry were very interested in economic ventures that involved both trade and production or plantation development. Gentry were simply satisfied with the competitive rents they were bringing in; and merchants were not interested in the delayed profits, risky investment, and unregulated nature of colonial and West Indies economic development prospects (Brenner, 1993, 110–112). Thus a vacuum existed, which would be increasingly filled by these nascent entrepreneurs.

From this socioeconomic development grew a fundamental divide within England's social class structure: on one hand nascent entrepreneurs and landed class elements, who for their own respective reasons did not need or want to (or could not) rely on the Crown for privilege and support, fused in opposition to the Crown, while on the other hand, those merchants who continued to rely on the Crown for their exclusive privileges moved into a closer alliance with the monarchy (Brenner, 1993, 200–204). The social consequence of this economic transformation was to create an increasingly entrenched conservative coalition, that is, between the Crown and the merchant groups in London who exchanged political and financial patronage for commercial privilege, and an evolving liberal coalition made up of the "aristocratic opposition," "small London traders," "Puritan ministers," and "new-merchant groups" operating the commercial trades in America (Brenner, 1993, 275–276). The latter's growing social opposition and divide sprang from a conflict over property, arbitrary taxation and religious sentiments (Brenner, 1993, 183–242). Ultimately, it would push these increasingly liberal social elements into the second phase of their liberal development: demands for the rule of law to ensure property protection and a predictable economic environment.

For the nascent colonial entrepreneurs, as well as the middle class of traders and shopkeepers in London, a profusion of taxes and levies plagued their economic activities and production, which at times was compounded by the arrogation of their land. As the Levant Company solidified its symbiotic relationship with the Crown, it also effectively avoided these rising taxes on goods: "The new book of rates issued in 1635, which raised the levies on a wide range of commodities, left the Levant Company merchants relatively unscathed, as the Crown failed to raise the duty on either raw or silk currants" (Brenner, 1993, 283). This same state predation also impacted the gentry, seen through the Crown's implementation of various Acts and measures designed to prosecute enclosing, beginning as early as 1489 with the Act of 1489, which attempted to curb peasant "depopulations" (Martin, 1983, 144);

the Act of 1536, which allowed the state to "fine any person who had enclosed illegally since 1488" (Martin, 146); the "parliamentary confrontations with the Crown in 1628–1629 over the issues of unparliamentary taxation, forced loans, arbitrary imprisonment, and, above all, Arminianism and the persecution of Puritans" (Brenner, 1993, 148); and arguably most notably, between the years 1635 and 1638 when a large number of fines were imposed. Added to these measures was the state's attempt to employ greater powers of taxation in order to compensate for declining revenue (Martin 1983, 114–148).

Furthermore, the previous way individuals conceived of the metaphysical and its relationship to political authority, including the nature and source of political legitimacy, and the socioeconomic prosperity or calamity for which it was considered responsible, taken for centuries as almost axiomatic, was shattered, and in its place an entirely new articulation of the world emerged. This cognitive revolution set in motion a secular trend characterized by inquiry, knowledge acquisition, and improvement. The abolition of controls on the press in 1695, followed by a profusion of writing and publishing, discussion and debate in public places, which over time became increasingly political (including input into, and opinion and criticism of, politics), helped fuel this revolution and produce a degree of transparency previously unknown to the people (Tombs, 2014, 289–306).

The Crown's implementation of restrictive barriers on who could conduct business within some of the most lucrative industries, and the predatory enforcement that followed, including arbitrary fines and even approval to only those who could provide bribes in an acceptable amount, as well as the king's mandates inhibiting the introduction of new and advanced machinery, and caps on the number of employees which restricted development and added expenses, all resulted in the maturation of a liberal enterprising class with property-law interests, that is, emphasizing economic freedom and private property rights (Nef, 1968; Root, 1994, 141–159; Lipson, 1920, 179–181; Martin, 1983, 114–148). As a consequence, the imperative to establish the *rule of law* in place of the *rule by law* became paramount for these newly formed social elements.

The conservative and liberal social coalitions that had formed in opposition, stemming from both religious and legal grievances, founded the Civil War, and indeed the Glorious Revolution that would follow, highlighting the emergence of an interest and rights-based (entrepreneurial) class (see Brenner, 1993; Tombs, 2014). A "community of suffering," "common interests," and a "corporate identity" resulted in a "longing for freedom" that represented a politically conscious class (Lipson, 1920, 188–190). Charles I, who represented one of the last vestiges of English absolutism, in attempting to strengthen absolutist institutions to unprecedented levels, "was felled at the centre by a commercialized gentry, a capitalist city, a commoner artisanate and yeomanry: forces pushing beyond it. Before it could reach the age of maturity, English Absolutism was cut off by a bourgeois revolution" (Anderson, 2013, 140–142). The re-ascendance of imperious political institutions following the Civil War, led first by Charles and continued by James, formed the catalyst for the Glorious Revolution in 1688 (Tombs, 2014, 256–259). As Tombs writes, James was "more Catholic than the Pope" and "more authoritarian than Charles, and more brutal than any of his Stuart predecessors" (2014, 258). The final straw was likely the proclamation by James in 1688 that Catholics would be exempt from "discriminatory laws" and the birth of his first healthy son with Mary (who was given a Catholic baptism) shortly thereafter (Tombs, 2014, 260). The Glorious Revolution provided the final blow to absolutism, and replaced the once supreme political institution of monarchical absolutism with an elected Parliament (with an electorate consisting of even farmers and common urbanites) (Tombs, 2014, 263; 237).

England's economic transformation and subsequent social-entrepreneurial evolution at the turn of the eighteenth century created the conditions necessary for the ultimate triumph of liberalism: individual rights were advanced, exemplified in the creation of the Bill of Rights in 1689, "which enshrined right of petition, free debate in Parliament, freedom of election, trial by jury, the right to bear arms and frequency of Parliament, and . . . forbade extra-legal royal action" (Tombs, 2014, 307); political participation and a government superintended by the people was achieved through the Triennial Act in 1694, which "required general elections every three years" (ibid); and from the year 1714 Parliament would win its enduring supremacy over the king in that "no bill passed by both Houses of Parliament has ever been refused the royal assent since George I's accession . . . parliamentary statutes were becoming the highest form of law" (Tombs, 2014, 316). Indeed as Zagorin writes, Parliament "abolished some of the highest prerogative powers of the crown and struck down forever the system of paternal rule, with its infringement on vested property interests" (Zagorin, 1959, 395).

Thus, the emergence of a bourgeoisie in England was characterized by a long and sustained evolutionary process, founded first in its economic shift away from feudalism and toward capitalist tendencies and accelerated by its lack of legal institutionalization, which created organized opposition from below vying for essential protection: of property, economic activity and ultimately the individual. The first phase of liberal entrepreneurial development arose as a result of an ascendant capitalist logic and the growth of markets, which produced increasingly rationally minded entrepreneurial elements focused on investment, innovation, business growth, and efficiency. The second phase of liberal entrepreneurial development emerged as a consequence of the proliferation of private property and the continuation of the *rule by law*; this presented a fundamental contradiction between the socioeconomic and politico-legal spheres, resulting in pervasive state predation, and imposing heavy costs on the very agents driving economic growth. The third and final phase of this liberal evolution resulted from the entrepreneur's response to the lack of the *rule of law*: instead of forming symbiotic ties with the state purposed with acquiring immunities and privileges, they organized and protested against the state, and thereby induced political institutional change. The consequence was the creation of representative bodies, elected by the people, to ensure the permanence of the *rule of law* and its animating principle—the intrinsic value and rights of the individual (see Figure 2.1).

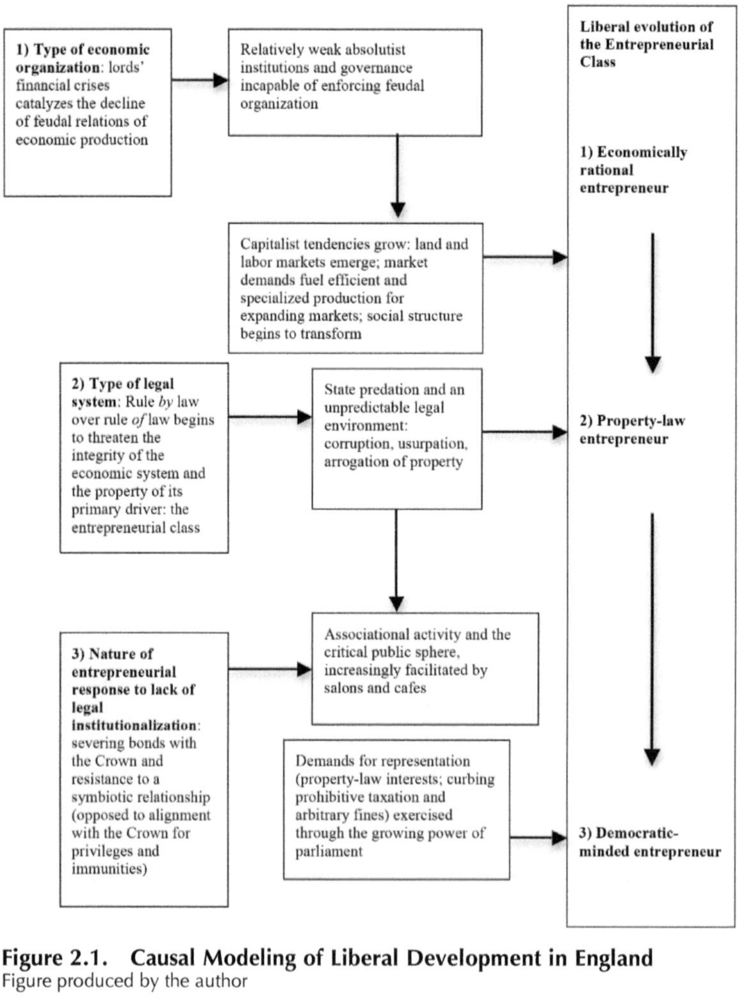

Figure 2.1. Causal Modeling of Liberal Development in England
Figure produced by the author

SOCIAL TRANSFORMATION IN FRANCE: THE DELAYED AND VIOLENT ROUTE TO LIBERAL VALUES AND INSTITUTIONS

The trajectory of economic development under feudalism, and then absolutism, in France, and corresponding degree of social evolution, deviated from the English experience, the divergence of which can be attributed to several variables: one, economic conditions were less conducive to capitalistic growth, including a less robust commercialization and the relative absence—early on—of lucrative markets. Two, French absolutism wielded considerable power, which not only influenced the course and degree of economic development (absolutism had a vested interest in maintaining the peasantry and preventing agrarian capitalism) but which also engineered the allegiance, if not outright dependence, of the nobility and emerging liberal elements. As hitherto mentioned, in England, landed elements and eventually urban entrepreneurial elements, with little enticement or co-optation from the crown, capitalized on emerging markets and in the process began to use land for production and profits, creating the conditions for a more peaceful and accelerated path to the modern liberal order. Thus, in England and France, the nobility and gentry responded very differently to the inevitable agrarian crisis, the responses of which were influenced by the prevailing incentives and constraints within each country (Root, 1994; Moore, 1966).

Prior to the eighteenth century, French society in general and the nobility and otherwise capitalist-oriented social elements in particular, lacked a similar degree of economic opportunity, which afforded the English nobility and eventual bourgeoisie such lucrative alternatives to feudal rent or the purchase of office. The wine trade, for example, although a major industry similar to that of wool in England at the time, only acted to buttress prevailing social relations within the feudal mode of production. Cultivation of grapes relied on labor and thus did not incentivize enclosure and the elimination of the peasantry, and although wine was widely produced throughout France, it was primarily consumed within its own borders. Furthermore, only one region—Bordeaux—was capable of yielding significant profits due to its proximity to waterways, and thus its advantages of transport. Even when economic opportunity did present itself, such as existed in the production and sale of grain, which eventually was produced in great quantity and was capable of being transported great distances, the fundamental structure of society did not change (Moore, 1966, 45–52). Incentives simply rested elsewhere. As Croot and Parker note: "this is not to deny that the rights of the French peasantry were an obstacle to more rational farming, particularly communal rights, but these would not have been an insuperable obstacle if the economic incentives and determination to override them had existed" (1985, 83).

The lack of economic transformation in France was also intimately connected to the strength of the political institutions of absolutism, including the incentives and constraints built into this structure. As Moore writes, "the monarchy wanted a prosperous nobility . . . as help in keeping people in their proper place . . . but the crown did not want the nobility to establish an independent economic base that could enable it to challenge royal power" (1966, 50). In England, lords effectively retained their (local) power, denying peasants legal rights to property through royal justice, displacing them through the process of enclosure, and creating the conditions for the development of land and labor markets; in France, absolutism ensured the persistence of a peasant-based agrarian economy managed by its partnership with the nobility. French peasants either acquired private property, or retained their "communal rights," and remained on the land in a way in which they did not in England (Croot and Parker, 1985, 83; Brenner, 1985b; Moore, 1966). French absolutism didn't destroy its feudal foundations or framework per say; it retained its fundamental structure, but redefined how one joined the ranks of the nobility, which under these new arrangements could be acquired through, most notably, the purchase of office (Skocpol, 1979, 52–57).

The sociopolitical consequences of these two factors became abundantly clear: although France may have possessed a landowning class with large holdings, and in certain areas (such as Normandy) with an economic efficiency that existed in England at the time, it lacked a similar enterprising and capitalist class (which also meant the continuation of a peasant-based agrarian order) with the objective of producing for the market (Cooper, 1985), and thus any hope for the maturation of a political bourgeoisie. In England, the strength of markets, and their potential for wealth, as well as a lack of political-institutional opportunities for wealth, provided the primary incentive to pursue economic efficiency and productivity; in France the landowning classes were drawn to the state for wealth (through the sale of offices), not to the market, and used any large holdings and economic efficiency to increase their own rents (Cooper, 1985). Instead of investments in techniques and production, and greater efficiency and output, declining agricultural productivity set in, a situation further exacerbated by squeezing of the peasantry and (heavy) state taxation of agricultural production.

One consequence of this political environment was the domination of a peasant-based economy, which, characterized by small holdings and a lack of specialization, and dictated and increasingly squeezed and taxed by French absolutism, inhibited growth (Skocpol, 1979, 55). As Skocpol notes,

> In France there existed a precarious balance of rights between a large small-holding peasantry, which owned outright approximately one-third of the land, and a landed upper class, which also had considerable property in land and possessed surviving seigneurial rights that could be commercially exploited. Thus, neither group was placed in a situation in which revolutionizing agricultural production was simultaneously to its interest and within its capacity. Innovation was also discouraged by the heavy burden and irrational modes of collection or royal taxes, which fell mainly on the peasantry (1979, 55).

Even the most commercially minded landed elements simply tightened the squeeze on the peasants opposed to the English counterpart who instead pursued greater efficiency and innovation of production (Moore, 1966, 52–53). Since peasants were primarily concerned with their own consumption, those practices in England which facilitated greater efficiency in production and greater output, such as investments in new tools and production methods as well as equal emphasis on pastoral and arable farming, were not prioritized, and as a result grain production decreased in the middle of the sixteenth century (Brenner, 1985, 307–308). As Brenner notes: "from the early sixteenth century, the peasant grip on production was clearly responsible for stifling the growth of output" (Brenner, 1985, 307). In fact, production continued to decrease despite the rise in grain prices. Failure to focus on livestock rearing, which was imperative for both the use of manure and ploughing to counter the increased use and potential deterioration of soil, meant that production in France would suffer. Pastoral and arable for the dominant peasantry in France were not complementary but instead in competition with each other, and arable prevailed. As noted earlier, even where large farms formed, these continued within the context of peasant, subsistence-based agricultural production. The economic divergence from the English course of development meant that France would once again experience a crisis which involved high prices, stagnant or declining production and the failure to produce what was required for subsistence (Brenner, 1985, 307–308).

The persistence of absolutist political institutions ensuring the existence of a peasant-based agrarian economy meant that the nobility and property owners had to find ways of ensuring sufficient and predictable income under these conditions. Many, as Lefebvre notes, simply turned the screws of feudalism tighter:

> Most lords confined themselves to demanding their feudal rights with a new rigor, a turn of events called the feudal reaction. They farmed out their rights to bourgeois agents who were relentless in collection of dues; they had minutely detailed manor-rolls drawn up, putting into effect dues which had become obsolete; they prevailed upon the king to issue edicts allowing them to appropriate a third of the common lands or to enclose their own fields and forbid the peasants to pasture their animals in them (2005, 14).

Yet many also resorted to extra-economic avenues for generating income; many diversified their investments and streams of revenue (purchasing of office, property, feudal privileges). The sale of office was a necessary vehicle for both the nobility and the monarchy: it was imperative for the continuation of the French monarchy, which was preoccupied with wars that demanded a near infinite stream of revenue; and it afforded privileges and immunities to the nobility, including commercial elements turned noble, and even became inheritable (Skocpol, 1979, 57–59). Wars had become increasingly costly not only due to longer periods of war but also due to more expensive methods and equipment, all the while the Crown was receiving less revenue due to declining agricultural productivity (Hilton, 1985; Croot and Parker, 1985). This mechanism was also imperative for the state in engineering the support and subordination of any potential social opposition, as well as for generating revenue, which at its apogee represented some "38 percent of royal revenue" (Anderson, 2013, 94–95). The state needed a healthy and predictable revenue to finance its ambitious military campaigns, while the nobility and bourgeoisie—in light of their crisis of revenue—benefited not only from fiscal privileges but also from military conquest—and the wealth that came from these ventures, including the capture of wealthy families (Brenner, 1985b, 269). Indeed, this symbiotic relationship with the state persisted for nearly a century and a half. As Anderson writes:

> It achieved the feat of integrating the nascent bourgeoisie into the circuit of the feudal state. For the purchase of offices represented such a profitable investment that capital was perpetually diverted away from manufacturing or mercantile ventures into a usurious collusion with the Absolutist State. Sinecures and fees, tax-farms and loans, honours and bonds all drew bourgeois wealth away from production. The acquisition of noble titles and fiscal immunity became normal entrepreneurial goals for *roturiers.* The social consequence was to create a bourgeoisie which tended to become increasingly assimilated to the aristocracy itself, via the exemptions and privileges of offices. The State, in its turn, sponsored royal manufactures and public trading companies which, from Sully to Colbert, provided business outlets for this class. The result was to 'side-track' the political evolution of the French bourgeoisie for a hundred and fifty years (2013, 99).

Another mechanism for ensuring both dependence on the Crown and a source of revenue was to provide nobility with lucrative positions within the church. Thus, whether it be the advantages of squeezing the peasantry or granting lucrative positions within political institutions, the Crown was for a time able to retain a loyal social base in the upper ranks of French society (Moore, 1966, 44–48).

Despite the myriad of creative ways the French state found to generate revenue, by the eighteenth century its revenue stream could not keep up with the financial demands of war. The expansive reach of the absolutist state, and accompanying powers (much of which were exercised through the growing class of *intendant* enforcers), nearly peaked by the seventeenth century, and by the eighteenth century, the situation had reached a tipping point, at least from the perspective of imminent revolutionary actors: peasants saw higher rates of taxation; nobility and gentry lost much of their autonomy within provinces and local institutions; and the privileges once enjoyed by nobles were terminated (Anderson, 2013, 96–101; Skocpol, 1979, 52–61). In the meantime, the developments across the channel in England, specifically its accelerated and unprecedented economic development, had created a much stronger and wealthier nation. These developments were to ignite the dormant grievances of the nobility, gentry and middle-class elements, against absolutism (Anderson, 2013, 1–111). As Skocpol writes:

> When its unquenchable penchant for war carried the eighteenth-century Bourbon monarchy into an acute financial crisis, it faced a socially consolidated dominant class. This class was dependent upon the absolutist state and implicated in its international mission. Yet it was also economically interested in minimizing royal taxation of its wealth and capable of exerting political leverage against the absolutist monarchy through its institutional footholds within the state apparatus (1979, 64).

The withering away of privileges and the increasing predatory nature of French absolutism, resulted in the growth of a newfound—and liberal—philosophy among French bourgeoisie, or the propertied and capital-owning social elements, and by the eighteenth century even began to subsume elements of the aristocracy (Anderson, 2013, 109–111). Capitalist ways had slowly seeped through the old order, detaching nobility from the Crown and positioning them in opposition to the absolute power of the king. Although the strength of the French autocracy for many years had successfully atomized a critical public sphere, preventing an early vibrancy that had existed in England (Habermas, 1989, 67–68), a critical public sphere emerged in France around the middle of the eighteenth century, which came to represent newfound liberal ideas, articulate in its philosophy, and purposed in its objectives to check the abuses and predation of absolutism. The social organization that emerged within the growth of towns, and forged a public sphere of critical discussion and organization, also founded the revolutionary and liberal ideas that would come to define the process of political-institutional transformation—and the activity in the cafés and salons came to reflect this emerging public sphere. The emerging bourgeoisie, initially represented by clergy, nobility, and relatives of Louis XVI, united in opposition to the aristocracy, and discussed the emerging principles of the day: religious freedom, equality of conditions, and overall liberation from political institutions (Lefebvre, 2005, 46–47; Moore, 1966, 84; 105).

The reconvening of the Estates General was a pivotal part of the process of Revolution in France. The Estates General provided the forum through which a growing number of social strata would identify and debate the core principles of the revolution, namely who would be represented and the particular characteristics of their newly envisioned national government (Skocpol, 1979, 64–67). The model of market relations—that is a legal superintendence of exchange relations based upon contracts—provided a template for exchanges in the political sphere: individual status and privileges based on estate and birth were no longer recognized (Habermas, 1989, 75). These deliberations first took place among the elite classes, the "professionals (especially lawyers), office holders, and intellectuals" (Skocpol, 1979, 176), but were soon joined by a diverse range of social strata ("artisans, shopkeepers, journeyman, and laborers" (Skocpol, 1979, 66)), including middle-class elements, demanding the rule of law and its universal application (not to exclude the highest officials or officials of the land). Although the "bourgeoisie" in the French case were not represented by a dominant middle class of capitalist-minded entrepreneurs such as existed in England (Skocpol, 1979, 174–177), the conceptual catalyst for the Revolution was similar to that of England: those possessing wealth and private property grew incensed over political institutions that arbitrarily raised and levied taxes, and threatened their property (Skocpol, 1979, 64–67).

The Revolution of 1789 began the process of political institutional change, creating a domino effect that would slowly topple the autocratic institutions and replace them with institutions representing the emerging bourgeois society:

> The Jacobins broke up the ground in which feudalism had been rooted, and struck off the heads of the feudal magnates who had grown there. Napoleon established throughout France the conditions which made it possible for free competition to develop, for landed property to be exploited after the partition of the great estates, and for the nation's powers of industrial production to be utilized to the full. Across the frontiers he everywhere made a clearance of feudal institutions, in so far as this was requisite to provide French bourgeois society with a suitable environment upon the continent of Europe (Marx, 1926, 24).

Constitutional development following the Revolution mandated a new legal framework for all to acknowledge: the constitution of 1791 stated, " 'the free communication of ideas and opinions is one of the most precious rights of man. Everyone can therefore speak, write, and print freely' " (Habermas,

1989, 71). Furthermore, "the constitution of 1793 explicitly included freedom of assembly in the protection of freedom of expression: 'The right to communicate one's ideas and opinions, whether through the press or in any other manner, the right to assemble peaceably . . . cannot be refused' " (Habermas, 1989, 71). In turn, "among bourgeois of diverse kinds was forged a link that nothing could shatter—a common detestation of the aristocracy" (Lefebvre, 2005, 46). Foundational to their detestation of the aristocracy was its refusal to acknowledge, in Moore's words, "equality before the law," "private property" and the "rights of man" (Moore, 1966, 84, 105), principles which for the first time transcended those of hereditary identity, official status, or political power.

France presents a unique—yet illuminating—case of socioeconomic and political transformation. Whereas in England economic transformation was led by increasingly capitalist-minded entrepreneurial social elements outside of the Ancien Regime, resulting in a slow evolution of first agrarian revolution and then capitalist and industrial development, in France this process—to the extent that it existed—was led by the Ancien Regime, leading to a very different socioeconomic outcome (Moore, 1966, 109). Initially, landed elements and nobility remained or turned conservative, rather than liberal, and thus aligned with the state. When state coffers dried up and desperation set in, the state began antagonizing even those conservative elements historically supportive of it. If, when these elements turned on the state and clamored for their own rights and amelioration from state predation, they had not required the inclusion of other sectors of society, or if these social strata were not interested in the principles governing this growing dissent, the result would either have been rights exclusively awarded to elite ruling class elements (in line with conservative revolution) or the continuation of the status quo. Instead, there were enough middle-class propertied social elements also motivated by similar grievances to support and participate in its Revolution, which, in the end, ensured the triumph of liberalism.

CONCLUSION

The evolution of liberalism in England depended first and foremost on a new economic sphere and a new form of economic organization, particularly, a turn away from feudal modes of production and a move toward capitalist logic and methods, driven first by fiscal crisis and then by emerging markets and their opportunities for profit. Land and labor markets, efficiency and innovation, and mechanization and labor-saving methods of production defined this new economic sphere. In England, a severe crisis of income for the nobility, coupled with a relative weak English absolutism, or at least one that would not reinforce the prevailing feudal order by inserting its direct control over its institutions, motivated landed classes to embrace capitalism. Society, particularly social class structures, thus began to transform, becoming more rational from an economic perspective, and less ideologically dominated by the state, paving the way for a new—and potentially powerful—philosophy. The consequence of this first phase was to produce a propertied class outside of the ruling class establishment and governing bodies, and thus, the evolution of liberalism's second phase: the realization that the *rule of law*, over the *rule by law*, as essential to the protection of property, capital and the individual. Pervasive state predation, including prohibitive taxation and arbitrary levies and fines, founded these interests. The final result was the demolition of traditional political institutions and the ascendance of representation, individual rights, and the rule of law.

In the case of France, the first variable necessary for the evolution of liberalism—that of a new form of economic organization—failed to take root. This is explained in part due to a lack of economic incentives to transform this sphere, and in part by the ability of French absolutism to double-down on retaining the prevailing feudal framework. As a result, new life was infused into a very old socioeconomic system, and the social class structure changed very little. Nevertheless, the fiscal demands of constant war forced the French state to scour the land for new ways to generate revenue. The sale of offices—a form of co-optation—initially proved beneficial to the state, and to officeholders, to whom privileges and legal immunities were provided. These individuals wed with the state to avoid predatory fiscal and legal policies, unlike their English counterparts. This not only prevented any politico-legal opposition to the rule by law, but it also ensured that resources would be earmarked for the state and not for economic investment. At first, the sale of office, in addition to collecting taxes directly, proved sufficient; but over time new forms were required. The result was a level of state predation that even encroached on the nobility, causing irremediable revolt from above. This process seemed headed for a conservative outcome, likely generating results for the ruling elite alone. Instead, possibly because of the minor ways in which the economy and social class structure did change over nearly two centuries, a diverse spectrum of social elements outside of the established ruling class joined the movement, and by doing so ensured that the foundation would be set for an eventual liberal outcome. The revolution of 1789 effectively toppled long-standing traditional political institutions and began the process of implementing institutions that reflected an end to political monopoly, the *rule by law*, and privileges based on one's status.

Chapter Three

Illiberal Class Development in China

907–1976

This Chapter analyzes the rise and fall of China's entrepreneurial class from the Song dynasty through the Moaist era, highlighting the variables that contributed to periods of socioeconomic growth, stagnation or decline. China began its socioeconomic ascent into the modern world centuries before that of the West, particularly that of England. The Song dynasty produced an agricultural revolution and a number of incalculable innovations that mark this period as one of the most prosperous in Chinese history. Tragically, with the rise of the Ming, this progress was stopped in its tracks; even worse, it was reversed by many degrees, before economic stasis set in, lasting until the fall of imperial China in 1911. What could explain this withering away of one of the most prosperous epochs in Chinese history?

China's lack of socioeconomic development prior to the Chinese Revolution of 1911 meant that conservative actors, the ruling elite that is, would drive the movement and dictate its outcome. The consequence was the emergence of a politically vacuous environment, filled increasingly with provincial militarism and warlordism. Although a bourgeoisie emerged in Shanghai by the mid 1920s, conditions were such that the expansion of their newly formed liberal paradigm was impossible, and indeed, destined to fail. They initially aligned with the KMT, hoping it would both assume political control over the nation and support the liberal interests of this class; instead, the KMT turned on the bourgeoisie, before suffering defeat at the hands of the CCP, producing grave political consequences for the possibilities of a new—and widespread—Chinese liberalism.

The Maoist era initially brought restoration to the lack of political order that China had faced for decades, through the consolidation of a national authority in the CCP. Notwithstanding this consolidation of political power, and the relative peace and stability it brought, this period of calm proved short-lived, as Mao began to articulate and employ his vision—the mass line, or mass campaign and mass mobilization—for achieving the socialist transformation of China. Mao's vision of purifying society and inducing revolution by galvanizing the masses first meant the liquidation of the bourgeoisie, which Mao pursued through mass campaigns. These campaigns, particularly the Five-Anti Campaign, cleared the way for modernization through mass mobilization, manifesting in the Great Leap Forward (GLF) and descending into the equally devastating Great Proletarian Cultural Revolution (GPCR).

The GLF was an important turning point, in that it signified a departure in the Chinese leadership from a unified to an increasingly divided body—primarily arising from a difference of opinion on what caused the GLF to fail so miserably. Liu and Deng represented the pragmatic faction that wanted to revitalize the economy even if this meant having some market elements; Mao and other top officials, on the other hand, represented a radical view that would not tolerate the growing revisionist elements inside the party. The events that unfolded demonstrated Mao's keen ability to build a majority faction against the pragmatists, and unleash the GPCR in an attempt to deal the final blow to remaining elements of the bourgeois society inherited from pre-revolutionary times. The consequences were not only catastrophic for the bourgeoisie, but for the nation as a whole—its economy, society, and polity. These periods provide key points of comparison to contemporary China, and help illustrate why post-1978 changes have produced an environment increasingly favorable to the emergence of a new Chinese liberalism.

CHINA'S SOCIOECONOMIC TRAJECTORY: 907–1911

Unlike Europe, China lacked a long-standing history of feudal institutions, and experienced some thirteen centuries of an autocratic state between its partial feudalism under the Zhou and its economic transformation and agricultural revolution under the Song (Von Glahn, 2016, 13). To the extent that China was "feudal" it was only so as late as the Zhou dynasty, and, arguably, only partially feudal. The Zhou dynasty was characterized by its "partrimonial rule," and governed China under a type of split system, whereby the west was governed directly by the Zhou ("royal officers"), and the east governed indirectly (by "archer lords") (Von Glahn, 2016, 12–17). These "archer lords," and the sphere in which they ruled, resembled something akin to European feudalism:

> The domain rulers gained full authority over their subjects and the fruits of their labor. They owed fealty to the Zhou king and often were called upon to

> provide military assistance . . . the archer lords were first and foremost military commanders, but held dominion over their territories, whose inhabitants were subject to their lord's juridical authority and demands for revenue (Von Glahn, 2016, 17).

This, though, was likely the extent of any sort of Chinese feudalism. Thus, although it was previously believed that the Tang/Song period witnessed the rise of the manorial order similar to Medieval Europe (see Elvin, 1973), recent scholarship has refuted the claim that a manorial order existed where peasants were enslaved: in China, especially by the Tang/Song period, landlords (imperial kinsmen, wealthy families or officials) who owned landed estates oversaw either tenant farmers, who largely operated independently, or hired labor. Indeed, as Von Glahn notes "The Song repealed older laws that had subjected tenants and hired laborers to the arbitrary control of landowners" (2016, 219). The significance of this, for land and labor markets, and overall economic growth during the Song, cannot be overstated.

The Song dynasty (c. 907–1279) produced the most robust and growth-oriented economy in the roughly three thousand-year history of Imperial China. The Song dynasty's economic revolution, for one, was founded upon unparalleled technological advancements in farming techniques and the introduction of new strains of rice, which spurred developments in transportation and specialization, and increased overall output. Advancements could be seen in preparation of the soil through advanced knowledge and tools, wider application of fertilizers, and advancements in hydraulic techniques. Furthermore, the invention of woodblock printing allowed for the production of agricultural manuals, which facilitated the spread of new ideas and methods of production. The fact that producers could sell their surplus, coupled with the continued growth of markets, encouraged specialization, and in turn greater efficiency (Elvin, 1973, 114–130).

Infrastructure expansion, particularly construction of dams and reservoirs, dredging projects, and the development of transportation routes over both land and water, all helped extend agricultural production, commercial networks and long distance trade. Developments in water transportation proved most impressive at this time. In fact, as early as the Tang dynasty, China "had 2,000 boats built for service on the Yangtze. Each had a capacity of about 50,000 kilograms, so together they carried almost a third of the total carried by the British trading fleet in the middle of the eighteenth century" (Elvin, 1973, 136). The Song vastly improved the construction and integrity of its ships, seen through the use of iron nails and waterproofing methods, among other advances, which with the invention of the compass in 1119, improved maritime strength (Elvin, 1973, 131–138; Ebrey, 2010, 142–144).

Fundamentally underpinning these unprecedented developments was the fact that under the Song dynasty statutory land and labor obligations were abolished—despite the traditional Chinese aphorism: '"king's land, king's people"' (Mio Kishimoto, 2011, 71)—as well as the fact that landownership had become "nearly universal" (Von Glahn, 2016, 252). This, in turn, released the productive energies of the people: the peasantry metamorphosed from subsistence producers to entrepreneurial-minded specialized producers for expanding markets—both domestic and foreign. Inter-province trade included rice from one region for oranges in another, for example (Elvin, 1973, 128–129), and regions which produced rice most efficiently would trade their excesses for a host of other items, including "incense, candles, spirit offerings, cooking oil, salt, soy sauce, vinegar, flour, noodles, pepper, ginger, and medicines" (Von Glahn, 2016, 266).

This demand extended beyond China's borders, which, with the aforementioned advances in maritime capabilities and the lack of commercial hostility from Song leaders, gave way to a vibrant international trade, and fueled growing trade with other East Asian nations. In particular, the maritime trade helped fuel commercial growth by facilitating the export of local commodities, namely ceramics, and the import of products in demand, namely cotton from India and timber and sulfur from Japan (Von Glahn, 2016, 270–272; Elvin, 1973, 171). As a result of these economic advances, China rapidly urbanized. For example, in one prefecture in the twelfth century roughly 6 percent of the population was considered urban; by the middle of the thirteenth century this increased to roughly 28 percent (Elvin, 1973, 175), leaving Elvin "to conclude that China at this time was the most urbanized society in the world" (Elvin, 1973, 177). Indeed, Von Glahn notes that the Southern Song boasted urbanization levels that approximated the levels that existed in Europe centuries later (Von Glahn, 2016, 250–251). This unprecedented economic revolution, though, tapered off by the fourteenth century (Wong and Rosenthal, 2011).

General consensus is that China failed to build upon the economic growth previously achieved under the Song, and instead remained in a highly commercialized yet static economic state (see Elvin, 1973, Wong, 1997). The reasons for this economic stasis, and subsequent absence of social-structural transformations (i.e., the rise of a bourgeoisie) in late Imperial China, can be attributed to the particular incentives, and constraints, which were present at the time, and how they dictated the activities of a growing population. For one, the nature of China's political system created strong incentives for individuals to aspire to a position within the bureaucracy (which on the whole did not exist in England). The Chinese bureaucracy wielded a most unique, and certainly comprehensive and absorbing political mechanism, which attracted social elements through its promise to provide status, wealth, and power: the civil service examination system. China's civil service examination system, which endured from 589 CE to 1911, served as an incredibly strong incentive. It promised an enormous amount of privilege through the power and prestige that accompanied the degree-holder, thus prioritizing political advancement over greater economic productivity and efficiency, and the creation of wealth. Its expansion during the Song is no coincidence considering the agricultural and commercial revolution which occurred during this period, as well as the external threats the Song faced—particularly at its northern border. The examination system was purposed with cultivating officials in the Confucian way, which prioritized service to the people and loyalty to the state (in other words it co-opted potentially divisive elements such as powerful merchant-entrepreneurs) while also purposed with preventing a dominant military elite (Ebrey, 2010, 112; 145–147; Chaffee, 1986).

As a result, the examination system assimilated these social elements before they could develop into potential opposition (Shigeta Atsushi, 1984, 343; Elvin, 1973, 92). Not only did the examination system "absorb the energies and the ambitions of the able and condition them ideologically through the curriculum at their own expense" (Elvin, 1973, 92), but it also "absorbed groups rising from below into the bureaucratic stratum and in the process obstructed new class organization" (Shigeta Atsushi, 1984, 343). The incentives which fueled this system were powerful: even at the high point of China's economic success, such as under the Song, individuals, even communities, devoted an impressive amount of resources to help family members or other community members pass the exams, since passage provided protection and privilege—especially protection of accumulated wealth—that otherwise could not be safely secured (Chaffee, 1986, 186–187).

These degree-holding scholar-gentry, and most notably official-gentry, accumulated capital through a wide range of privileges (Shigeta Atsushi, 1984): fiscal immunity, especially taxation; collection of extra-legal fees; legal immunity, specifically a system whereby only a limited number of superior bodies or individuals could prosecute given infractions (Chu points to a law which stated that only the emperor himself could prosecute his officials); and access to land, to name a few (Chu, 1988, 168–192). Accounts of families, whose members passed the *shengyuan* (the scholar-gentry), and more significantly, the *jinshi* (the official-gentry), demonstrate the monetary benefits involved: as Chang notes, after the brothers of the Tseng family passed the *shengyuan*, their incomes improved markedly, and skyrocketed after gaining entry into the official-gentry world (Chang, 1962, 7–8). In terms of taxation, there was a great distinction between levels of taxation imposed on gentry and those on the rest of the people. Gentry paid less than what the law prescribed, whereas remaining social groups paid legal rates plus additional fees, creating prohibitive levels of taxation (Chu, 1988, 168–192).

The real wealth that they accumulated derived not from official salaries, which were quite low, but from extra-legal taxes collected, contributions and gifts or "customary fees," which although illegal, were widely acknowledged and approved practices, so long as they were kept within "customary limits." For example, in *Kiangsi*, although a magistrate's annual income was 1,900 *taels*, his average income after the aforementioned streams of revenue averaged around 30,000 *taels* (Chang, 1962, 7–8; 39). Furthermore, legal immunities allowed them to expropriate property or other forms of wealth, including land grabs or graveyard seizure, collecting taxes on main transportation routes especially on rivers, or extra-legal taxes at county fairs. Those affected had little recourse to legal means, since laws limited the extent to which gentry could be prosecuted, a law which even protected immediate family members (Chu, 1988, 178). Thus, China's civil service examination system was a virtually unparalleled system of assimilation that incentivized individuals to join the bureaucracy and in this process reduced the desire to find alternative avenues for elevation, namely economic avenues.

The opposition of certain Chinese emperors and political elites toward commercial and industrial growth also acted as a force pushing back the tide of socioeconomic change and growth. Examples include the Han official Yin Shang, Ming Taizu, and emperor Gaozong of the Qing dynasty. During the Han dynasty and under the watch of Yin Shang, merchants who failed to register were buried alive, while commerce on the whole was highly restricted and regulated (Elvin, 1973, 165). Ming Taizu, who came from a very impoverished background, was considered one of the most autocratic emperors and one who vehemently promoted an agrarian order. In order to achieve this ideal, he set out to decimate the market economy that had sprouted under the Song, which included reversing the trend of privatization of land that had previously predominated. Furthermore, he proscribed all foreign maritime trade, and replaced it with China's long-standing tribute system, which set China back some 150 years (Von Glahn, 2016, 285–287). The unprecedented achievements produced during the Song, including the compass, by this time were being utilized to the fullest by European powers to facilitate expanding trade networks with East Asia, all the while China was embracing an agrarian order unconcerned with the kind of economic productivity which could grow its economy. The Qianlong emperor of the Qing dynasty, similar to Ming Taizu, also carried a certain degree of opposition to commercial activities, especially with foreign nations, witnessed in his famous exchange with Lord George Macartney (Brook, 1999; Ebrey, 2010, 209–216; 235–236).

Some scholars have pointed to evidence of prohibitive levels of taxation on commercial and industrious activities, as well as the sanctioning of monopolies (Mann, 1987, Holt and Turner, 1966). During the Qing dynasty, liturgical organizations took the form of merchant guilds, which were given substantial powers by the state, as we will see below in the review of the salt monopoly and the Co-hong. Their power included "limiting competition," "the power to assess and remit commercial taxes," and the ability to dictate the terms and arrangements of trade (Mann, 1987, 23–24). The state benefited in this symbiotic relationship in two ways: it was guaranteed an inefficiently organized yet sufficient revenue stream, and the monopoly that it sanctioned ensured limited if any economic growth. Here we see the state's continued emphasis on the agrarian order. The state was not interested in supporting merchant activities, but instead on controlling and limiting their growth. As Mann writes, "market regulation, not revenue, remained the primary concern of early Qing rulers" (1987, 45). The merchants, for their part, benefited in this relationship by being awarded exclusive rights to trade, and as a result, they reaped massive profits. These arrangements of course are most evident in the prominent monopolies, but this arrangement also existed at the local levels: "as far as the government was concerned, members of the local elite . . . could even contract to pay commercial taxes and use them as weapons for parapolitical control—limiting access to the market by competitors, and protecting their own assets from the government's squeeze" (Mann, 1987, 95).

Other scholars have pointed to a connection between monopolies, informal taxation, and economic growth. Although three main areas—the salt monopoly, foreign maritime trade, and money lending institutions—are typically highlighted, the state also controlled a number of other industries. During the Ming dynasty, the state controlled the production of much of what its own elite consumed, including "armories, textile factories, metalwork shops, leatherwork shops, saddlery shops, paint shops, apparel factories, [and] wineries" (Holt and Turner, 1966, 106). The state also monopolized production of commodities most widely consumed and demanded throughout society, including iron, salt, tea, matches, silk, wine and tobacco. As Holt and Turner note, these "were the prerogative of the state and not an unrestricted preserve for private investment and entrepreneurship" (ibid). When and where the government did allow private investment and involvement, these activities were highly regulated, which included the state reserving the right to confiscate the final product at artificially low prices (ibid, 107–108).

The salt trade was one of the most prominent trades in China, including in the late imperial period. By the nineteenth century it was second to the land tax in terms of the amount of revenue it generated for the state. This amount of tax revenue, the additional large contributions these merchants made to the state, and their lavished lifestyle, all support the notion that this monopoly was highly lucrative (Chang, 1962). The salt trade was a 43,500,000 *tael*, per annum, business (after taxes), an amount of which was shared by only a few hundred gentry-merchants (Chang, 1962, 190), comprised of about 30 "head merchants" (*zong-shang*) who supervised the remaining "small merchants" (*san-shang*). The administration of this trade was overseen by the salt censor, under which were a variety of functionaries including the salt commissioner, salt intendant, a number of deputy and assistant commissioners, inspectors, treasury staff, salt receivers, examiners, and clerks (Ho, 1954, 131). Furthermore, it was structured and controlled in a way in which the state determined who had control over production and distribution (these two areas were in many cases controlled by separate parties) and even prescribed market areas and specific transportation routes for each respective distributor. Transporting or selling outside of these routes or market areas was strictly prohibited (Chen, 1914).

Through the distribution and sale of salt one can begin to observe the degree of state regulation, and the exclusive nature, of this monopolized trade. Salt was conveyed through either private or public monopolistic structures, though the private monopoly seems to have predominated. Under the private monopoly, "introductory certificates" were issued to those who were able and willing to pay a large sum of money in advance, regardless of their future salt sales. On this certificate a number of items were listed, including "The name of an assigned market." Once this was obtained, the merchant then had to obtain a "bill of drawing," which stated that a certain individual may buy a certain quantity of salt, at a certain field, and during a certain period. Finally, the merchant had to obtain a "waterway ticket," which indicated the specific route that must be used to transport the salt as well as the specific market destination. Finally, each salt producer or salt-producing area was given a specific salt-consuming territory and market in which to sell salt, and transportation or sale of salt across these lines was strictly prohibited (Chen, 1914, 70–92).

The very nature of this monopoly limited those who could participate in the production, distribution and sale of salt, and in turn limited competition, creating salt prices and an overall trade which benefited these privileged gentry-merchants at the expense of the consumer and overall economic expansion. This appeared to be a very symbiotic relationship: the state asked the thirty or so head merchants to both oversee taxation of the trade and also to monitor the actions of the other two hundred and seventy or so merchants, and in turn, the state promised to sanction their exclusive rights to production, distribution, sale and ultimately profits generated from the business (Brandt, Ma, and Rawski, 2014). Here we can see the necessity of gentry status to enter into one of the most lucrative trades at the time. As Ho notes, the salt merchants were those who successfully achieved gentry status, and from this status were then able to "pay the salt gabelle in advance . . . the right to sell salt, being an inalienable one, was commonly called *ken-wo*, literally 'rooted nest' " (Ho, 1954). Thus, first and foremost, entry into the salt trade was reserved for the limited finite number of people who were able to successfully pass exams or find a way to purchase a degree.

Foreign maritime trade also reflected the monopolistic structure seen in the salt trade. As noted earlier, foreign trade in China was eliminated in the beginning of the Ming dynasty and was only revived in limited fashion in the early part of the nineteenth century. In particular, foreign trade was limited to the port of Canton, and was circumscribed by the guild known as the *Co-hong*, which regulated entry and determined the conditions of business. The government sanctioned this guild, which consisted of thirteen merchants, to oversee these activities, and as a result of these exclusive rights to foreign trade, these merchants enjoyed significant profits and amassed large sums of wealth (Holt and Turner, 1966, 108–109; Chang, 1962).

The merchants and their guild ensured that entry into the trade was limited and tightly controlled. Any merchant wishing to enter the trade had to produce a written document verifying his tax liability, a document which also had to be confirmed and signed by each fellow merchant member. Furthermore, similar to the salt trade, there was an initial fee to join the *Co-hong*, which had to be paid prior to entry, and which was in the neighborhood of 200,000 *taels*. Evidence also points to additional entry fees, particularly the common "customary fee" which averaged 42,000 *taels*, 55,000 *taels* for tribute to the emperor, 20,000 *taels* for repairs on the Yellow River, and 130,000 *taels* to purchase presents for the emperor; emergency contributions, which averaged 70,000 *taels* annually; and import and export taxes which were estimated at 1,000,000 *taels* annually. These taxes and fees were of course a significant liability for the merchants, though they passed these impositions on to others, probably primarily to producers, foreign merchants or entering members of the guild (Chang, 1962).

Government regulations, which were strictly enforced, clearly stated that all foreign trade, whether exporting tea or silk or importing foreign goods, must pass through the *Co-hong* merchants in Canton. The customs officials were entirely unsympathetic to the prohibitive charges imposed on goods coming into China, in part because a large portion served as a revenue stream for officials and the state, and in part because of the state's anti-commercial attitudes. As the governor of Kwangtung and Superintendent of Customs noted: "if the foreign merchants thought they could not make a profit by trade, they could stop coming for trade" (Chang, 1962, 164). Once the monopoly on foreign trade in Canton had come to an end in 1842, and the five treaty port system was established, officials continued to effectively force the flow of commodities through Canton; when commodities made their way through one of the other four ports, officials effectively imposed the tariffs which would have applied if the goods had shipped through Canton.

Some scholars have also contended that levels of taxation further blocked the sort of economic breakthroughs which were developing in Europe. Overall, taxation in late imperial China fell disproportionately on non-gentry elements, particularly merchants and peasants. As mentioned previously, the gentry secured a profusion of privileges, one of which was autonomy to control their respective localities. Indeed, magistrates required the help of gentry in order to effectively control the locality; this included powers of taxation, which in many cases were abused. As Chu writes, the notorious *yamen*, or "runners," who were typically impoverished and marginalized citizens, were employed to collect taxes on behalf of the magistrate. In many cases the magistrates simply did not compensate these runners, and as a result the runners resorted to extra-legal taxation, or outright confiscation, in order to support themselves. Thus peasants, merchants, and even wealthy landlords, who were not fortunate enough to garner gentry status, were unable to wield the political power required to avoid these predatory actions, actions which arbitrarily extracted capital that could otherwise have been used more efficiently, at least certainly in economic terms (Chu, 1988).

Probably the most significant tax, in terms of its impact, was the *lijin*, which was the first major formal tax implemented outside of the land tax. It was a tax on commerce introduced in the nineteenth century, and became a very burdensome tax, with bureaus established at many points along trade routes waiting to tax goods. Its introduction has been attributed to the state's desperate need to find new streams of revenue due to unexpected financial burdens, in particular the Taiping Rebellion, and other internal conflicts. Nonetheless, consistent with previous ideological positions and economic policy, many officials at this time decried the presence of merchant profits and surpluses; the *lijin* tax, and its impact as an arbitrary obstacle to further economic growth, can thus also be seen as a direct move to limit profits. To be sure this was not a novel concept in China; as early as the Chou dynasty commerce was regulated through excise taxes not for revenue but for regulatory purposes (Chen, 1914, 93). In fact, the mentality of the creator of the *lijin* tax himself intended for this tax to constrict trade, and incentivize people not to engage in the world of commerce, but to remain on the farm (Mann, 1987, 102–103).

The *lijin* tax was applied to various phases of commerce, particularly production and transit. A tax was first applied to the inventory in warehouses or shops, and then also applied when goods were in transit, which were especially destructive to the development of the economy. In the city of Jiangmen, for example, the *lijin* tax was implemented soon after the expansion of its economy, which devastated the economy and reversed its previous economic growth. Trade, which had been growing, and which was expected to continue to grow and eventually compete with other major trading centers in Guangdong, simply declined following its implementation. Between the introduction of the *lijin*, and the privilege conferred upon merchant monopolies, Jiangmen, which was not strategically situated along major trade routes in the way that Canton, Chaozhou and Wuzhou were, could not possibly compete. This *lijin* tax delivered the most deleterious blows to those merchants outside of any corporate identity, guilds or otherwise, by not only taxing the same commodity up to five times, but also in the way that these taxes delayed trade (since much of this area depended on riverine trade). As one merchant described:

> When merchants invest their money in merchandise, they have to pay a local tax (*luodi shui*) when they make their purchases, and entry tax (*jinkou*) when their goods arrive, a "situ" (*zuogu*) tax while the goods are stored, and exit (*chukou*) tax when they take them out to sell, and transit taxes at each lijin bureau on the road. When you tax the trader's place of business and his inventory, you already reduced his capital; when you then tax both his cargo and his shipping, how can he hope to make any money at all? (Mann, 1987, 141).

However, recent scholarship has opposed the argument that heavy taxation, monopolies and state intervention were stark, at least prior to the eighteenth century, and were major factors in reversing China's socioeconomic advances under the Song (Wong, 1997; Wong and Rosenthal, 2011). As one scholar writes, China collected "most of its taxes without encouraging rent-seeking activities or giving local-level officials much opportunity to create autonomous bases of power and authority . . . there were few monopolies, low tariffs, and a well-developed separation of economic and political powers" (Wong, 2012, 354). Instead, research has shown that China's divergence was due to very different conditions, and thus incentives, governing the behavior of China's elite and entrepreneurial elements (Wong and Rosenthal, 2011).

The incentives which prevailed in China, and in contrast to Europe, in addition to the factors listed above in the civil service examination system and the general hostility of elites and emperors toward commercial and industrial activities, were largely determined by the interrelated variables of war and scale of empire. In Europe, constant warfare both fragmented the territory while also creating a constant need for the state to find sources of revenue to fund military activities. This impacted several features related to economic and political development, most notably, reliance on capital or labor for production and type and degree of taxation (Wong and Rosenthal, 2011).

First and foremost, war created very different incentives in Europe particularly in the area of production, which had lasting socioeconomic and political consequences. Considering the relative absence of threats, China had little incentive to move production to urban areas and the protection and security they afforded, and to shift to a reliance on capital; on the contrary, the abundance of labor and peace in the countryside meant that labor was valued over capital (Wong and Rosenthal, 2011). Indeed, "Chinese entrepreneurs did not usually need to anticipate that warfare would disrupt their production and distribution operations" (Wong and Rosenthal, 2011, 112). In Europe, constant threats, and the resultant warfare, facilitated both urban and capital intensive development. With endemic warfare, the means of production in rural areas become severely threatened, particularly capital, since it is vulnerable to arrogation. The response to this was to move production to a location that can reasonably protect capital and production activities: urban areas, protected by walls (Wong and Rosenthal, 2011, 99–110). Furthermore, greater attraction and concentration of manufacturing in urban areas, which experience relatively high labor costs and low capital costs, due to a higher cost of living and guilds, results in a reliance on capital over labor (Brenner, 1993, 36–37; Wong and Rosenthal, 2011, 109–110). As Wong and Rosenthal note, "it was this capital bias that set Europe off on a different path toward machine-based innovation: urban manufacturers in Europe created more machines than their rural Chinese counterparts because they had more use for them" (2011, 110).

Thus, probably the most influential variable, created by the relative peace in China and relative instability in Europe, was the reliance on capital in Europe and the reliance on labor in China for production. China was ahead of Europe in terms of technological and commercial development until around 1300 C.E., but from 1300 onward stasis set in, while Europe experienced rapid development. The main reason behind this is the fact that Europe, which became increasingly urbanized, along with this also increasingly relied on capital over labor for production, while China, which did not experience rising levels of urbanization (after the Song dynasty), continued to rely on labor. China saw a decline in urbanization from 1300 onward: whereas as much as 7.5 percent of the population lived in an urban environment in 1300, by 1900 this figure is estimated as low as 3 percent (Wong and Rosenthal, 2011, 111).

Furthermore, despite the aforementioned types and periods of taxation and regulation in China, on the whole taxation in China was light, a condition which also stemmed from the relative absence of threats. For one, although evidence exists of local magistrates engaging in corruption, including extra-legal taxation and harassment by local runners, on the whole taxation was low. In addition, in many cases wealthy individuals took responsibility for funding public services in their respective localities, which helped curb both local revolt and excessive taxation. Moreover, due to constant threats facing European states, more than 70 percent of revenues were devoted to responding to threats or preventing these threats from materializing, while in China the emperor was able to devote more than 50 percent of his revenue to other causes, including the public's needs. Furthermore, when analyzing taxation as a proportion of the nation's GDP, even the highest rates of taxation in China were still significantly less than England or the Netherlands, and even less than that of France (7 percent) (Wong and Rosenthal, 2011, 175–182). Moreover, taxation after the Song dynasty (which taxed both commerce and agriculture) was limited primarily to agriculture until the end of the Qing dynasty, which taxed agricultural production (but not handicraft production) at under 10 percent in most areas. To be sure these rates did rise near the end of the Qing dynasty, from about 1850 onwards, particularly seen in the *lijin* tax described above, but this was a reflection of sheer desperation for revenue on the part of the Qing regime due to the rapidly expanding nature of internal and external threats, and forced indemnities. The Taiping and Boxer Rebellions had effectively ended the peace and stability that China had enjoyed for centuries (Wong, 2012).

Thus, the absorbing and potentially lucrative nature of office-holding within China's bureaucratic machine, the shift in policy following the Song/Yuan period, particularly the commercial opposition employed by Ming Taizu (reversing Song policy on privatization of land; proscribing maritime trade) that set in motion a reversal of the progress achieved under the leadership of the Song dynasty, coupled with relative peace, which produced a desire to rely on labor and a lack of incentive to invest in capital, all contributed to the fabsence of liberal class development. Moreover, for the same reason that labor was relied on over capital—relative peace—the state was able to avoid heavy and arbitrary taxation and levies, and in doing so, avoid the type of state predation that produced a liberal entrepreneurial class *for itself*, in the legal and political sense of the term, in the West. The ephemeral glimmerings of an autonomous, interest-based entrepreneurial class following the fall of imperial China, would eventually face utter liquidation in the wake of Mao's socialist ideology and economic policies.

THE REPUBLICAN ERA AND AN EPHEMERAL CHINESE BOURGEOISIE

The Chinese Revolution of 1911 was the result of growing disaffection with the political authority among the localized gentry. The politically tenuous environment that persisted in post-revolution China can be understood not only in light of the lack of China's modernization, but furthermore, in the provincial influence underlying the revolution. The Chinese Revolution, and its political consequences, were derived from a string of interrelated events founded upon economic factors: China remained engaged in localized commerce, not industrialization. The peasants, which were maintained on the land as the productive forces, instead of replaced to make way for advanced production, while also increasing in number, were also subjected to proliferating and pervading gentry corruption. As a result, China experienced peasant rebellions in the nineteenth century, which crippled the imperial authority both militarily and financially, and which in turn forced it to contract military power out to the localized gentry power bases. This reinforced a growing system of provincialism and gentry factionalism. In the end, the reforming efforts initiated by the Qing from 1898 to 1910 acted mainly to reinforce the segmented institutional power in the localized gentry, while diminishing its power (Skocpol, 1979, 67–79). Thus, what emerged was an unpredictable economic environment, an arbitrary legal environment, including taxation, and a veritable degree of political instability (Bergère, 1983; Wen-hui Tsai, 1986).

Though the end of the revolution was met with high hopes for China's future—with intentions to install constitutional and representative institutions—the reality was that the characteristics of China's periodization following the revolution were far from conducive for the realization of this end (Skocpol, 1979, 79–80). Sun Yatsen's Republic, characterized by its emphasis on abolishing privilege and monopoly, as well as increasing modernization, was established in 1912 as the national government (Bergère, 1983). Nonetheless, its short life—ending the same year—saw the rise of a dictatorship in the regime of Yuan Shikai. This commenced the degeneration of the political environment, and the subsequent decline in a supportive business environment for China's entrepreneurial class. As an editorial in a Chinese newspaper notes in 1916 stated, "The merchants have their business calculations upset. This condition of affairs will, if not amended, very likely cause universal dissatisfaction amongst both Chinese and foreign merchants. Yuan should bring himself to understand that all these evil consequences have been caused simply and solely by his unbridled ambition" (The *North China* Herald (NCH), 1916a, 251). Subsequently, although it seems that the government apparatus under Yuan provided temporary support for and stability behind business activity, in the spring of 1916, a social impulse began to grow for his resignation (NCH, 1916c). As a newspaper article noted,

> So far the anti-Monarchist movement has only caused a suspension of business activity in certain regions, and has not led to the wholesale destruction of the machinery of government which characterized the revolution of 1911. Provided a settlement is arrived at speedily such a condition may be almost entirely avoided. But every day during which the situation is allowed to drift makes a recovery more difficult (NCH, 1916b, 376).

On the eve of Yuan Shikai's death in 1916, China's political environment began to splinter as warlordism ensued, and in turn, created large-scale destruction to the economy and its potential for growth. Warlords increasingly exploited all areas of the economy: they forced peasants into military roles; imposed arbitrary rights to all farming operations and possessions; and placed high taxes on goods (NCH, 1919a, 5; Fairbank, 1986, 180). The Qing dynasty had actually provided a main driving force behind the creation of warlords, and their provincial militarism: due to the ineffectiveness of its military in managing both domestic and international threats, they assisted provincial officials in establishing their respective military forces, which in turn, fostered not only the rise of competing bases of power against the Qing, but after its fall, the rise of warlord governance (Wen-hui Tsai, 1983, 33–34).

Thus, accelerating growth in China's coastal regions, especially Shanghai, was met by a highly unsupportive political environment. In turn, China's economy and entrepreneurial class, though continuing to grow, remained isolated in the coastal areas, and ultimately dependent on foreigners. As an article on Shanghai markets noted in 1916, "conditions in the country are such that good demand is confidently looked for. Merchants and dealers are ready to buy, and the only thing that is holding back order just now is the unsettled state of China politically" (NCH, 1916d, 402). China's key resources remained untapped, while foreign nations capitalized on China's underdevelopment: Japan, for example, developed trade with Manchuria (in place of China), exhibiting "energy, inventiveness, and skilled organization" (NCH, 1916e, 427). This environment of instability depressed economic growth on a national scale, and in turn, prevented the rise of markets, industries and entrepreneurs. An article at the time noted:

> The world today is full of distressing losses and bewildering opportunities, both of which are apparent on every page: and it is deeply to be regretted that the stupidity of China's political upheaval which is chiefly to blame for the former has also prevented her from taking more advantage of the latter than has been the case. Here for example is a passage which ought to make Chinese officialdom blush, if it have not wholly lost the faculty for doing so: "Piracy on the Canton River was not quite so frequent, owing to the policy of establishing patrols and garrisoning dangerous localities. But the North River was still so unsafe for native craft that most of the freight has been diverted to the railway. Junks only travel in fleets, and engage "soldiers" who are supplied by agents guaranteeing a safe passage. The junks pay, it is said, a fee of 5 percent of the value of their cargo, and the agents pay the pirates to leave them alone" (NCH, 1916e, 426–427).

World War I brought new opportunity for China's industrialization: new markets were opened to Chinese opportunists and industrialists with the decline of foreign presence; and imports decreased significantly, creating a void especially in markets such as cotton products. By the end of the war, and with circumstances advantageous for China's continued growth, such as a return to international norms in pricing and transportation, the Chinese business class revived its drive for native, societal-led industrialization. The sprouting of modern industry, linked to access to advanced machinery, was witnessed in areas such as the growth of cotton and subsequent construction of cotton mills; the growth in food industries and subsequent flour mills; and the rise of the tobacco industry (Bergère, 1989, 64–83). In 1913 China had 484,192 spindles and 2,016 looms; by 1919 it had 658,748 spindles and 2,650 looms (Bergère, 1989, 71). In May 1916 it was estimated that China had 27,500,000 *mu* of land devoted toward this industry producing an estimated quantity of 1,630,500 piculs (NCH, 1916e, 427); and by 1919, the evidence indicates not only the accelerated growth of the cotton industry, but one increasingly driven by Chinese entrepreneurs. Entrepreneurs were intent on moving away from consumption of imports and instead on developing domestic industries to supply growing demands (NCH, 1919b). As a newspaper article noted in 1919, this reflected a "change of old ideas," most importantly, the rise of the rational Chinese entrepreneur—the first phase in the evolution of liberalism—in capitalizing on the opportunities, and the potential for profit, in China's rising cotton industry (NCH, 1919c, 550):

> It was assumed and freely expressed a few years ago that it was only a matter of time when the whole of the Chinese mill industry would be in the hands of the Japanese. There are today big foreign and big Japanese interests in the established mills, but the development which has taken place during the past six months has been practically exclusively Chinese and when the mills, which now have been ordered and some of which are already in course of erection, are all accomplished facts, the Chinese themselves will have by far the predominant interest in the cotton mill industry of this country. This is due to men like H. Y. Moh, C. C. Nieh and C. C. Yung who have tackled the problem in a most businesslike and far-seeing manner, and by interesting their countrymen having the necessary capital, they have established a lead for the Chinese themselves (NCH, 1919d, 551).

By the end of the second decade of the twentieth century, the Shanghai entrepreneurial class indeed emerged independent of foreign influences. Although foreigners had controlled China's ports, most notably Shanghai, by 1919 native industrialists managed to successfully break the control of the foreigners and establish their respective businesses. The Nanyang Brothers' Tobacco Company is but one example: establishing its first branch in Shanghai in 1917, and faced with considerable odds, its persistence in development eventually yielded dividends: by 1919 the company had managed to open two additional branches in Shanghai and Ningbo alongside its foreign competitors (Bergère, 1989, 73–74).

The rise of the rational entrepreneur, catalyzed by this environment of economic freedom and accelerated economic growth which began to emerge at the close of the second decade of the twentieth century, collided with the lawless state of provincialism and militarism, and dominant warlords, who regularly disrupted the economic environment and the lives of businessmen (Bergère, 1983, 777–778). The result was the gradual formation of an entrepreneurial class with property-law interests—the second phase in the evolution of a liberal entrepreneurial class. As Bergère notes, a direct link existed between the effects of state predation on entrepreneurs and the development of their legal principles (1989, 219). As one entrepreneur noted in the North China Herald:

> We have two governments claiming supreme authority over the entire country, but in every province . . . an independent government has been set up which is governing without law or reason. Taxes are being levied by all of the governments and by individual commanders without authorization from anybody representing the people. . . . Civil wars have interfered with the means of communication and we are unable to bring our goods to markets where they are needed (NCH, 1921, p. 151).

Indeed, entrepreneurs showed signs of class association and organization, based upon these interests, and with the objective of finding a political solution to a lack of legal institutionalization—albeit confined to specific areas. In 1907 the Qing dynasty first established the Chamber of Commerce—the pillar of business interests. Although the intention of the Qing authorities was to establish this network of business organization in order to regulate this class' actions (a system of corporatism), the business class used this organizational platform to its advantage: they transformed what was associational activity ultimately dependent on the state, to activity independent from the state and with the objective of furthering class interests—especially in areas such as Shanghai, Guangzhou and Hankou (Strand, 1989, 100). In fact during the Chinese Revolution and thereafter, the Chambers of Commerce in Shanghai increasingly supported the business class and the ambitions that stemmed from their growing political initiative. Furthermore, associations such as the China Cotton Millowners' Association, the Association of Modern Bankers in Peking, and the National Bankers' Association formed in order to further the interests of the business class (Bergère, 1983, 732–733; 757–759). As Bergère writes, "they adopted a viewpoint of an international capitalism dominated by the themes of growth, progress, and competition" and produced publications devoted to discussing these topics. Indeed, "class interests took on a modern aspect. Solidarity was no longer—as it was in the guilds—the solidarity of interests acquired, but rather that of interests to be acquired" (1983, 759). Although this activity largely occurred in Shanghai, other cities such as Beijing also experienced the rise of associational activity among the business community (Strand, 1989, 16–17).

China political environment at this time, characterized by political instability and pervasive state predation, led not only to the development of an entrepreneurial class with property-law interests, but also one with incipient signs of liberal political values—the third and final phase in the evolution of a liberal entrepreneurial class. The following speech by a representative of China's rising bourgeoisie in 1921 in the *North China Herald* exemplifies the existence and liberal maturation of this class:

> Faced with a situation such as this [state predation, disrupting property and business], it is now the time for the merchants to renounce a time-worn tradition of not participating in politics. It is our task now to proceed immediately to participate in the affairs of state . . . we deserve and shall have an efficient and democratic government. Our difficulty lies in the fact that the middle class of China, the merchants, bankers, educators and industrialists, have not participated in the government . . . if we insist upon our rights as free men and as taxpayers, politics will soon enough become clean. . . . Are we slaves and traitors? I say no! The merchants of China will save this country (NCH, 1921, p. 151).

He then continued by stating:

> As citizens of the state it is our duty to participate in government. To fail to participate means to renounce our citizenship. As citizens of the state we must support our government when it is efficient and upright and we must criticize our government when it is inefficient and treacherous. In supporting or criticizing we are performing a political act . . . politics means the exercising of one's rights as a citizen of his country. That is the first duty of every citizen of a republic. . . . In no man can we have faith. No man can be the saviour of China. The people of China themselves must save the country. And we representing property, learning, position, must take the lead in indicating to the people the path. If we fail there is no hope for China. For who shall dare to lead when we have failed? (NCH, 1921, p. 151).

By the early 1920s, a Chinese bourgeoisie had emerged—in particular in the growing metropolis of Shanghai. They came to represent the product of decades of socioeconomic transformation, from the advent of economic freedom and the rise of Chinese industry, to the emphasis on private property and legal institutionalization as a result of state predation, and ultimately the embodiment of a liberal political philosophy: political representation

(Bergère, 1989; 2009). Nevertheless, as a result of warlord governance, liberal society remained isolated and with very little potential for expansion. As a newspaper noted in 1919, peasants turned to banditry in the rural areas and entrepreneurs were unable to extend their liberal paradigm, including organization and community, outside these localities (NCH, 1919a, 5). And as one observer summarized: "If China had a government whose word was indeed law throughout the country . . . practically all her troubles would disappear; only to ask for it seems like crying for the moon" (NCH, 1919e, 784).

Thus, the rise of a liberal entrepreneurial class would prove ephemeral when, out of desperation, it allied with the KMT, and the KMT would emerge as China's temporary—and illiberal—political authority. To understand their support for the KMT, as one motivated by China's long-standing cultural impulse to support the authoritarian state, is to miss entirely the structural developments that had evolved by the 1920s. Social elements had emerged that came to represent the heart of a liberal entrepreneurial class—a class in pursuit of specific legal and political principles. Although they contended with imperious authorities at the time, they also understood the necessity of a coherent and expansive political system, and one that served the interests of the people, particularly maintenance of, and support for, economic systems and a stable and peaceful society (Strand, 1989, 284–285). Chinese society had been plagued for years by unstable national political authority and unchecked foreign intervention, which in part factored into their rationale behind an emphasis on a strong state. Thus, the foreign influences, which in many ways became associated with interventionism and imperialism, were also a factor in the course of China's illiberal development (Lin Chun, 2006, 206).

The entrepreneur's alignment with the KMT was a desperate attempt to restore China's socioeconomic and political order in general, and in particular, the hope of establishing those interests fundamental to their existence: protection of private property, economic predictability and stability, and political representation. Although Chiang Kai-shek—whose conservative wing broke from the left-wing Wuhan faction—was initially an ideal representative for Shanghai's capitalists, his arbitrary actions at extracting money from them revealed an unchanging political situation. As Coble notes, the example of one of Shanghai's wealthiest businessmen is representative of the terror imposed on the emerging bourgeoisie. When Fu Tsung-yao realized the increasingly exploitative nature of the KMT regime, and subsequently refused to hand over capital, his private property was taken from him and he was forced to flee Shanghai. Fu Tsung-yao was only one of a number of capitalists who experienced similar arbitrary acts of intervention and confiscation by the KMT (Coble, 1979).

To exacerbate the situation, the KMT formed alliances with underground gangs, which increased the amount of arbitrary fines, extractions and taxation placed on the business community. As the relationship between the KMT and the Green Gang (particularly Du Yuesheng, head of the Green Gang) evolved, created from the lucrative monopolization of the opium trade, the Green Gang's power increased exponentially. For the bourgeoisie, this meant the gang's complete control over the business world (Bergère, 2009, 213–241). Nonetheless, under the leadership of the Finance Minister, T.V. Soong, the bourgeoisie had become politically active and conscious as a class, making their interests known and refusing to concede to the increasingly predatory environment (Coble, 1979). They attempted to utilize their financial power, and the insolvent state of the central government, to broker a deal that supplied the state with necessary funds in return for political reforms. When that failed, they attempted to convene a National Convention, initiated by the Federation of the Chambers of Commerce, to devise a national constitution and establish a national political authority; lasting no more than two months in Peking before falling victim to a coup, the bourgeoisie resorted to what proved to represent a final state of desperation: a move toward secession from China altogether along with the General Chamber of Commerce (Bergère, 1989). But in the end, they were effectively left with two options: localized provincial politics, or support for authoritarian regimes in the KMT and CCP.

The economic vitality of Shanghai between 1917 and 1927, including the use of the printing press and other means such as libraries to disperse the newfound precepts of modernity, facilitated the transformation of this great metropolis and created the conditions necessary for the evolution of an entrepreneurial class into an identifiable bourgeoisie (Bergère, 2009, 242–284). Nevertheless, the expansion of this liberal paradigm was dependent on a national and stable political authority and governance, necessary for continued economic growth beyond China's coastal enclaves, most notably Shanghai. The bourgeoisie's support for the KMT was out of desperation to find and restore this stability and order, hoping that what followed might secure the legal and political interests they required. The KMT never fulfilled the role that the bourgeoisie envisioned when it consigned its support to this revolutionary party; instead, corruption and lack of development persisted (Bergère, 2009, 177–212). The Sino-Japanese War as well as the Civil War (between the KMT and CCP) would perpetuate this instability until the rise of the CCP a decade later. Yet with its rise to power in 1937 and the promise of a national and stable political governance also came a political authority hostile to all things capitalist.

THE ELIMINATION OF THE PRIVATE SECTOR AND THE LIQUIDATION OF ALL REMAINING LIBERAL ELEMENTS

The communist takeover in 1949 signaled an impending transformation of China's socioeconomic organization. The party had specific socialist ideals in mind, and from 1949 on, the party attempted to merge China's social actors (peasants, workers and bourgeoisie) into one cohesive unit and nationalize its authority over them, and it would use mass organization and mobilization to achieve these goals (Teiwes, 1987). Indeed, through a series of campaigns Mao would not just merge—but effectively crush—the entire entrepreneurial class and eliminate the private sector.

The party first targeted the international bourgeoisie—the foreign capitalists and feudal agents (Mao, 1969, 417–418; Mao, 1954, 13–20; Mao, 1951). This tactic, as well as the overall rectification campaign and revolution, founded upon Chinese communism and Mao Zedong Thought, were influenced by Soviet-led communism and proletarian revolution. As Stalin noted in 1927 in a speech, "the first stage . . . of the revolution was leveled chiefly at foreign imperialism, the distinguishing mark of the second stage is that the revolution's spearhead is aimed mainly at internal enemies, primarily at feudal landlords and the feudal regime" (Encausse, and Schram, 1969, 230). This, Mao believed, would help win over the rest of the peasantry and form an overwhelming supportive base of peasants and workers (Mao, 1977, 33–36). Thus, his vision centered first on class struggle between the workers and the international-feudal bourgeoisie before moving into the phase of class struggle between the workers and the capitalist bourgeoisie. Liu Shaoqi also acknowledges this strategy in a speech in 1949 where he articulates that the party should first focus on consolidating the worker-peasant social alliance, which when accomplished would demonstrate a strong powerful social base capable of securing communist power throughout China (Liu Shao-ch'i, 1969, 175–182). As a result, in 1949 the party targeted the KMT, who Mao believed represented the feudal ruling classes, as well as the landed elite, all of which had been in collusion with imperialist forces. As Mao stated, they are "the vassals of the international bourgeoisie, depending upon imperialism for their existence and development" (Mao, 1954, 13–14; Mao, 1951, 8).

China's capitalist class became the second target in Mao's campaign to purify society. This philosophy was designed to incrementally suppress the town-dwelling, urban bourgeoisie: first use them to the party's advantage, then suppress them through mass campaign, and finally, see to their complete liquidation in order to succeed in socialist reconstruction (Mao, 1969; Mao, 1951, 6–8; Mao, 1952, 11; Mao, 1954, 14, 20). The urban campaign that created the spark for the fire that would slowly engulf the entrepreneurial class was the *Wu-fan* (Five-Anti) Campaign—designed to control and eliminate the national bourgeoisie (Gardner, 1969).

Although from the start Mao exhibited political antagonism toward the bourgeoisie, indicated in his writings (1969), the party initially refrained from targeting the capitalists. This is where the party realized that it must capitalize on the skills, resources, and strength of the bourgeoisie to further strengthen its authority over China and the prospects for national development. In the party's first years it not only required support from the urban environment including a skilled workforce, but the party also had not yet demonstrated its authority over urban areas, such as the social and economic strength of Shanghai. Thus, its initial approach was one of moderation toward capitalist elements (Gardner, 1969, 478–479; 486). In fact, powerful leaders in the party made public announcements that signified a party tolerant of entrepreneurs' property and business. As Liu Shaoqi notes in 1950, "The people's government has not at present forbidden private persons to set up any enterprises which are beneficial to the people and do not exercise a dominant influence over the people's livelihood. . . . The people's government will give the necessary facilities and direction to those entrepreneurs who are honest . . . and will help them . . . to succeed in their enterprises" (Liu Shao-ch'i, 1969, 202–203). In the initial stages of consolidating communist forces it was important for the party to prioritize its agenda for consolidating its own power and planning the future of China (Mao, 1977, 33–36). As Liu Shaoqi made clear, in the interim period this would include entrepreneurs (1969). Nonetheless, the party would, over time, suppress and subordinate the following three social elements: those associated with capital and property, those associated with Western education and values (including professionals), and finally, the intellectual community (Whyte, 1991). This approach followed an incremental process, a process that would consolidate its social base and eventually install socialism. In 1953 private industry still produced 66 percent of all output; by 1957 this would diminish to under 3 percent (Lardy, 1987, 157).

The party's ultimate goal, and final stage, was to eliminate capitalism and install socialism. In order to do this, they would move through the cities and reverse its transformation in private industry through a planned economy that would eradicate liberal elements, including entrepreneurs. (Mao, 1969, 364–372). The Three-Anti (designed to deal with cadres corruption), Five-Anti (designed to denunciate and manage bourgeoisie-corrupting tendencies) and Thought Reform (to mute the liberal thoughts of the intellectual community) Campaigns were all a means to achieve this end (Teiwes, 1987, 90). The implementation of the Five-Anti Campaign most evidently stemmed from the party's weak presence in and over China's urban environment, not to mention

Mao's paranoia over liberal remnants (Mao, 1977, 17). As Mao said in his 1949 address to the Political Consultative Conference:

> The imperialists and the domestic reactionaries will certainly not take their defeat lying down; they will fight to the last ditch. After there is peace and order throughout the country, they are sure to engage in sabotage and create disturbances by one means or another and every day and every minute they will try to stage a come-back. This is inevitable and beyond all doubt, and under no circumstances must we relax our vigilance (1977, 17).

The urban environment and its social actors in many ways still contradicted the ideology and goals of the CCP. The party's opposition to the socioeconomic forces in China's cities was related to a number of factors. It deeply mistrusted the forces behind China's urban evolution: those that had compromised with imperialism, and the bourgeoisie which had been generally supportive of the KMT. The party did not know how fully it could rely on workers' support in the cities until they had proceeded past the initial stage of "alienation and exploitation." They suspected that many workers maintained positive working relationships with the bourgeoisie (Gardner, 1969, 484; Mao, 1977, 106–107). Finally, increasing corruption in the cities and the leadership's inability to control this environment led to the adoption of more radical policies which manifested in the form of mass campaigns (Gardner, 1969, 495).

Intensifying corruption seemed to be the primary factor that produced and accelerated mass campaigns in the cities beginning in 1951 (Gardner, 1969; Mao, 1977; Barnett 1964). These campaigns were most specifically intended to "cleanse the Party and entire bureaucracy of 'rightist' deviations and 'bourgeois' thought" (Barnett, 1964, 138; Mao, 1977). As Mao argued in 1953 in response to bourgeoisie corruption of party cadres, and in the aftermath of the campaigns, "the bourgeoisie is sure to corrode people and aim its sugar-coated bullets at them" (Mao, 1977, 107). The Five-Anti campaign was aimed at the bourgeoisie due to their economic ties to the party bureaucracy, and more specifically, at eliminating corruption that resonated from bourgeoisie-cadre relations. To be sure, although corruption demonstrated a daily part of business life, particularly in Shanghai, any profit made by the business community was considered illegal and exploitative in the eyes of the party. Thus, in the end all reaches of the business community were targeted (Barnett, 1964).

In 1951 Mao made his concerns clear regarding urban China in general and the bourgeoisie in particular—articulating the corrupting connection between bourgeoisie and communist cadres—and subsequently orchestrated his campaign against the "five evils" (Mao, 1977, 64–70). In Mao's words, these were "bribery, tax evasion, theft of state property, cheating on government contracts and stealing economic information" (1977, 65). In 1952 Mao revised his initial view of the bourgeoisie—that of representing only a minimal threat to the party—and labeled them as the "principal contradiction in China" (1977, 77). As the March 1952 "Directive of the Five-Anti Movement" by Mao states, "In the past, this matter was treated with leniency. In the future it will be dealt with strictly . . . to industry, be lenient; to business, be strict. To ordinary business be lenient; to opportunists in business, be strict" (Mao, 1952, 11). By the middle of 1953 he would make clear the urgency in not only combating the "five evils" spreading from bourgeois foundations, but moreover that the bourgeoisie were a direct threat to the party line—to the success of socialism embodied in Marxism-Leninism ideology. In fact, by this time Mao would make clear—through his articulation of the failed opportunities in the past to successfully assimilate the bourgeoisie (KMT-CCP alliance; War of Resistance; and 1949 forward)—that in order to inculcate the principles of socialism to China's population, it would be necessary to depart from party-bourgeoisie relations (Mao, 1977, 103–111).

The party utilized several strategies to carry out the Five-Anti Campaign and to deal with the issue of urban control. This included first setting up a business association comprised of prominent bourgeois actors that needed little convincing to support the newly inducted communist regime. Second, the party used this group of loyal bourgeoisie to conduct various campaigns in order to diminish the power of the business community and subordinate them to the communist regime; this had little effect. The most effective method was the party's empowering of the workers. The party conducted campaigns to indoctrinate the workers into believing in a separate identity from that of the bourgeoisie. This tactic proved fruitful: it encouraged the workers, if literate, to read newspapers which revealed workers denouncing their employers; if illiterate, workers were provided the possibility of hearing propaganda through public broadcasts or public readings. The creation of small organizational units of workers, designed to denounce their employers and garner support from those who had not climbed on board, led to a greater breakdown of the bourgeoisie (Gardner, 1969). The catastrophic impact of the Five-Anti Campaign on China's private entrepreneurs cannot be overstated. Indeed as Malik writes, "those who could not stand the suffering committed suicide while the rest waited for the next attack and simply surrendered to the will of the government" (1997, 41).

The campaigns unleashed to target the bourgeoisie in the first eight years of communist rule acted to slowly liquidate this class in all its dimensions—economic, cultural, and ultimately political (Liu Shao-ch'i, 1958, 419–420; Barnett, 1964, 143–144). The rectification campaign had a catastrophic effect on the enterprising and entrepreneurial class: capital was reallocated from private business to the state, converting private enterprise into state-owned industry (Barnett, 1964, 143–144; Teiwes, 1993, 39–40; Chen and Chen, 1953); industrial and commercial activity vital to the success of business was halted; beneficial relations between cadre and bourgeoisie were severed to due cadre fear over punishment; and finally, it eliminated any political ambition on the part of the bourgeoisie (Barnett, 1964, 143–144). By 1956 China had in effect eradicated its liberal entrepreneurial population and significantly reduced the private sector (Malik, 1997, 41–43). As Chou Enlai stated in 1959, "As a result of the socialist rectification campaign, the Chinese people have repudiated bourgeois ideas and greatly raised their socialist and communist consciousness" (Chou En-Lai, 1959, 7). China's top leadership made sure that these liberal elements remained eradicated for the rest of Mao's reign. As Liu Shaoqi stated in a speech in 1958, at a time that marked the close of bourgeois liquidation campaigns and the start of the GLF:

> The experience of the rectification campaign and the anti-rightist struggle once again shows that throughout the transition period, that is, before completion of the building of a socialist society, the main contradiction inside our country is and remains that between the proletariat and the bourgeoisie, between the socialist road and the capitalist road. In certain fields this contradiction manifests itself as a fierce life-and-death struggle between the enemy and ourselves; that was the case in the attack launched by the bourgeois rightists in 1957. This attack was repelled, but in the future they will try to make trouble whenever opportunity arises. We must, therefore, be prepared to wage prolonged and repeated struggles against the bourgeois rightists before their contradictions with the people can be fully resolved (Liu Shao-ch'i, 1958, 420).

Following the famine in 1956, which resulted from Mao's collectivization policy and intent on eliminating property ownership, Mao began targeting, in the thousands, those who identified his problematic economic policy—and then accelerated this policy by launching the GLF. Peng Dehuai was one of the earliest high-ranking officials purged during the GLF for criticizing Mao's GLF policy; scores of purges of other officials followed shortly thereafter. Liu Shaochi, one of Mao's closest advisors, also became one of the many victims of Mao's campaign to cleanse the party of bourgeois elements, as Mao increasingly viewed him as a threat, which derived, fundamentally, from a difference over economic policy (Becker, 1996, 47–82). Indeed, as Becker writes, as early as 1950 Liu "was arguing in favour of protecting the property of rich peasants and against requisitioning surplus land" (Becker, 1996, 49) and at one point even criticized Mao over his preference for collectives. Mao believed that the GLF, which disposed of property ownership and scientists, and galvanized peasants into action, would realize unparalleled levels of production. This did not happen. Instead, subpar, unusable steel was produced, and grain production slowed. To be sure, Mao, and even Deng Xiaoping and Liu Shaoqi for a time, believed their methods were creating production on a massive scale. This was in part due to the fact that officials and peasants were feeding fiction and manipulated reports to Mao, which were also carried in official media outlets (Becker, 1996, 47–82). As a *Peking Review* excerpt stated in 1959:

> The expansion of the scale of agricultural production in China is unprecedented. Prior to the establishment of the people's communes, China's 120 million-odd peasant households organized some 740,000 agricultural producers' co-operatives which have now been reorganized into more than 26,500 people's communes. Each embraces an average of nearly 5,000 households with a labour force of approximately 10,000 and about 60,000 *mu* of land. Agriculture in China is still not mechanized and electrified, but the scale of capital construction in farming and water conservancy now being carried out by the people's communes, the shift from shallow ploughing and extensive cultivation to deep ploughing and intensive cultivation, the change from "big areas with small output" to "small areas with large output" and the intensive garden style cultivation of farmlands are something that does not and cannot happen in any capitalist country (Tung Ta-Lin, 1959, 6).

The inflated reports up the chain claiming widespread surpluses led the party to extract more and more grain from provinces which was then used for export or to increase domestic stock, while at times harvests were neglected for steel production that couldn't be used. In the end some 30 million would perish (Becker, 1996, xi; 47–149). The purges that began during the GLF would lead to an entire assault on the party apparatus in the unleashing of the GPCR, which would effectively end Mao's reign and set the stage for Deng Xiaoping's unprecedented economic reforms.

The campaigns in the 1950s and then the GLF and GPCR that liquidated all liberal elements in society and eliminated the private sector, had with them, extinguished any hope for a renewed Chinese liberalism. In 1952 and through the Five-Anti Campaign the party had suppressed the property-holding bourgeoisie; in 1956 the intellectual bourgeoisie were muted and on the eve of the GLF they were excluded from involvement in party led development; and in 1966, the bourgeoisie that had supposedly infiltrated the party had become the final targets as the GPCR was set in motion (on the GPCR, see MacFarquhar, 1974, 1983, 1997). The GPCR was a campaign that experimented with indoctrination on a national and comprehensive scale, and in turn, eliminated any remaining remnants of liberal thought. The revolutionary youth were the final instruments used to carry Mao's ideology and re-educate the party, and ultimately, with an aim to "achieve all-round ideological, political, economic and organizational victory" (*Peking Review*, 1968, 8). Thus, the GPCR was Mao's final card in his attempt to eradicate all bourgeois elements in China, which in this rectification campaign extended to the highest ranks of the party. Paradoxically, this final campaign would not only cause significant destruction to the fabric of the party, but it would also give unprecedented rise to the very liberalism that Mao so vehemently opposed, manifested in the ascension of Deng Xiaoping and his bold economic reforms.

CONCLUSION

Imperial China, especially by the time of the Ming dynasty, represented a commercially advanced society with extensive trade networks and technological advancements that transcended even Western progress at the time. But despite these inroads towards greater and unprecedented development, China's socioeconomic development halted, and indeed retrogressed, remaining stagnant from the early Ming through the end of Imperial China in 1911. Relative peace following the Song dynasty, Ming Taizu's hostility towards commercial and industrial development, and China's political-bureaucratic machinery, including its civil service examination system and its co-opting effects, all contributed to China's lack of sustained socioeconomic development. The Qing dynasty largely continued this hostility towards commercial activity and economic development, while internal conflict towards the end of its tenure fueled prohibitive taxation on commercial activity—and ultimately its demise. These factors, which limited China's economic advancement, produced distinct social and political consequences: China's social class structure remained predominantly peasant-based and lacked a large middle-entrepreneurial class-and its political system remained autocratic.

The forty-year period from 1949 to 1989 was a period of great economic, social, and political turmoil for China. The consolidation of the party's power in 1949 followed a period of complete social and economic exhaustion and a politically vacuous environment, filled with political instability and military aggression. The bourgeoisie that had emerged within the Shanghai metropolis and which had peaked in the 1920s, had to accept the rise of this new political authority. The bourgeoisie initially viewed this new political environment with hope; after all, the party issued a proclamation that it would allow the capitalists to persist without fear of class persecution. This would prove to be an erroneous assumption. To be sure, the first few years proved hopeful for the bourgeoisie. But it seemed that for Mao it was more of a way to use the bourgeoisie to solidify the party's—or his—power. If the bourgeoisie were viewed favorably, it wasn't by Mao, but by others within the party—such as Liu Shaoqi or Deng Xiaoping. As a result of Mao's distrust of the bourgeoisie and ideological opposition to capitalism, he employed his preferred methods of socialist reconstruction: mass campaign and mass mobilization. The outcome was the decimation of the bourgeoisie. The Five-Anti Campaign, in particular, not only demoralized the entrepreneurial class it crushed any remaining elements, and set a pattern in motion that would come to define the relationship between the party and China's property-owners.

The GLF and GPCR that followed would further destroy the social, economic, and political fabric of pre-revolutionary China. The GLF was an attempt to modernize China by following an economic model for development based upon Mao's socialist ideals: to use the power of China's masses to transform the nation. It proved to be a flawed approach in both its economic and political assumptions. In the aftermath of the GLF, Mao's closest advisors presented alternative methods to re-instill life back in to the economy—all of which, as long as they remained alternative to Mao's idealistic model, would be associated with revisionist policy. Thus, the GLF created the seeds for the GPCR four years later—the last of Mao's campaigns that would seek to weed out and reeducate the revisionist elements that he believed had sprung up around him.

Bourgeois society in China—as an economic, legal, cultural and political category—was eclipsed in the years of radical experimentation with building a socialist society. The turn to reform after 1989 has released the economic and social formation of a bourgeois society again, and indeed allowed it to reach unprecedented heights. But the bourgeoisie only exists as an economic and social thing in itself—as Hegelian/Marxian analysis (see Hegel, 1952, 1995) would put it—it is some way from being a thing for itself, lacking the political maturity and associational and legal forms that would allow us to say that China has a bourgeois society. Over the next three chapters this book explores the possibilities on full bourgeois transition.

Chapter Four

China's Private Entrepreneurs

Economic Rationality and Autonomy

By the end of the 1970s China was in ruins, due to Mao Zedong's obsession with socialist ideology and the mass line as a means to achieve his ideological ends: campaign after campaign slowly worked to undermine individuals, classes, and eventually the party apparatus itself, and in doing so decimated China's economy, social fabric, and political cohesion. As a consequence, China was left in a state of social and mental dissolution, and economic and political instability. In Deng Xiaoping's mind, the only solution was the party's embrace of a new form of economic organization, namely, one characterized by a sphere of economic freedom in which individuals could produce for markets, while employing labor and using land and capital, (theoretically) independent of state control.

As a result, this new economic sphere has transformed China's social structure and cleared space for the emergence of an entrepreneurial class, which begs the question: to what extent has this transformation produced a liberal entrepreneurial class, specifically, one that is economically rational and autonomous? The evolution of middle-class entrepreneurial elements both economically rational and autonomous was the first step in the evolution of a liberal entrepreneurial class in the course of Western development, and a necessary foundation for the evolution of a liberal class with specific legal—and ultimately political—interests. This chapter seeks to examine the extent to which China's entrepreneurial class is evolving along a similar liberal trajectory.

MARKET OPPORTUNITY AND THE RATIONALIZATION OF THE ENTREPRENEUR

A particularly notable feature of China's emergent entrepreneurial class is the quantity and quality of their growth within a culture that has historically viewed these social elements as specious, if not sheer pariahs, within society. Indeed, the fact that these social elements are not only growing in number but are emerging with rational characteristics—embracing market opportunities, innovating and creating businesses and new business ideas, and generating wealth—is especially significant. For example, a recent survey of 2,000 entrepreneurs revealed that entrepreneurs' primary reasons for pursuing entrepreneurial activity are in order to acquire wealth and gain independence. When asked "What was your main motivation in starting your own business?," 30 percent of active entrepreneurs and 31 percent of those seeking to become entrepreneurs said "to make more money," and 46 percent of active entrepreneurs and 51 percent of those seeking to become entrepreneurs said "to be independent and 'be my own boss' " (Gamester, 2011).

Survey results of private entrepreneurs published in 2005 in *Siying Qiye Fazhan Baoguo* (Report on the Development of Private Enterprise) also revealed similar responses and findings. When asked "what was the most important reason for establishing your private enterprise?," entrepreneurs responded in a rational way. Over 20 percent responded with "to achieve greater value in my life"; 16 percent responded with "the previous working environment did not allow for the development of individual abilities"; and 15 percent responded with "the compensation in the former work unit was too small" (Ao Daiya, 2005, 65).

A survey conducted in 2013 by China's *Zhongguo Jingji Shibao* (*China Economic Times*) concerning "enterprise managers' views, issues, and recommendations regarding the overall economic situation and enterprise management conditions," asked entrepreneurs their perspectives and opinions regarding the current (economic and market) situation. Results showed an emphasis on market reforms, improving their quality of life, privatizing the economy, and greater accountability of public institutions. According to the report:

> Entrepreneurs believe that the most urgent reforms are . . . related to marketization, including optimizing a fair competition market environment, streamlining the administration and instituting decentralization, and promoting the effective flow of private capital into the banking, energy, telecommunications, and railway spheres (2013).

Furthermore, the author's interviews with entrepreneurs revealed that they value economic freedom, and its expansion and protection, including opportunities presented in emerging markets—an indication of the growing rationalization of China's entrepreneurs. Some examples will help illuminate this phenomenon. One of the fastest growing markets in China is the mobile technology market—that of smartphones, tablets, and the like, and its submarkets. One entrepreneur, realizing the opportunities available, developed a particular mobile app in China that caters to the female population; as she told the author, there is an overwhelming number of mobile apps for men, but very few for women, so she created a mobile app for women—premised on the concept of pet raising. Her ultimate objective with this app is to foster brand advertising through the attachment between user and pet and their various interactions—such as coupon collection with an elephant's trunk. Important in this case is not only her creation of a mobile app, and the complexities of the design, but more so a recognition to target a specific and underrepresented demographic (Entrepreneur 17).

Another entrepreneur recently developed a business that targets an emerging market in China—a safe and high quality food supply. While discussing his business he noted "We are attempting to try all the new things that no one else has tried" (Entrepreneur 18). The significance in this case, as the entrepreneur revealed in a nearly four-hour interview, is the fact that his rationality extends beyond the identification and engagement with this market; his motivation also involves combating what he termed "the bugs" in China, or the connection between the one-party system and various unchecked abuses of political power (discussed in further detail in chapter 7). Although food safety issues related to Chinese sourced products are pervasive, as he explained, even in the well-known foreign supermarkets in China the food supply conditions can be precarious. In one example the claim was made that Carrefour (*Jialefu*) was selling a particularly toxic fish—called "Oilfish"—that they labeled as cod, which gained significant attention in the media and in China's growing Internet discussions (Ji Beibei, 2012). As he noted, this issue of food safety went viral after a famous Chinese actress (Ma Yili) was affected by the fish, who subsequently initiated a discussion on a microblog concerning China's endemic food safety issues; as is commonly the case with these sensitive issues, it spread rapidly (Entrepreneur 18; Ji Beibei, 2012). On the issue of corruption behind this phenomenon, or one of "the bugs" associated with the one-party system, as he put it, he conveyed that part of the motivation behind the design and creation of his business was to attempt to combat this problem. As he stated:

> Food safety is very bad in China. There are problems with regulation. In China you have to pay membership fees as suppliers, so fake products make it to shelves while real products are turned away—they call them channel costs. In China we have government departments to check food safety, but they are doing nothing. Every time they will wait for the complaints; if they don't complain

> they will sell and the trouble will continue. Even if customers complain they still won't do anything. The reason why this came to the fore, the Carrefour issue, is because it affected a famous star who posted this on Weibo. In China we cannot rely on government related institutions for food safety checks. The government institutions capitalize on profiteering and thus allow poor safety standards to continue (Entrepreneur 18).

Two Shanghai-based entrepreneurs the author interviewed succeeded by way of their own drive, ingenuity and determination, and acutely reflect this embrace of China's newfound sphere of economic freedom and opportunity. One particular entrepreneur the author interviewed has successfully established a Western themed restaurant business in one of China's major cities. What is interesting about this particular entrepreneur is his degree of success in this industry, and quick success, considering little personal or professional experience prior to opening his first restaurant. This restaurant has become a hot spot for expats: on weekends you'll wait at least an hour for a table; and during the week you'll be hard-pressed to find a table at lunchtime without a wait. He has recently opened a second location (after delay as a result of arbitrary government intervention), and with urgency, since as he noted—he must spread his restaurant's name before others identify his success and copy his model (Entrepreneur 9). The second example is an entrepreneur the author sat down with on multiple occasions. This particular entrepreneur essentially conjoins emerging start-ups that hold ideas and business models with significant potential, but that lack necessary resources, such as investors, equipment, and a collaborative working environment. His business is what is known as the business incubator. In early 2012 he opened a second location—four times the size of the original location (Entrepreneur 7).

One particular Beijing-based female entrepreneur commented on the prevalence of economic opportunities in contemporary China, especially as compared to the first decade of reform and opening up, as well as how many people are deciding to embrace these opportunities and take risks. In response to the question, "as a result of China's modernization, do you feel that a new mentality has emerged in China's entrepreneurs?," she noted:

> 10 or 15 years ago people if they want to start a business they choose a certain industry that they specialize in and therefore it is easy to do this; however now, because there is so much more opportunity today people will start a business in any given industry—even if they are very unfamiliar with it—in order to maximize on the potential rewards from this venture. So people today are much more brave to branch out and try new things. For example, in Shenxi Province there are many long-time miners who—although have no knowledge

of the film industry—have come to Beijing to set up businesses in this industry (Entrepreneur 2).

In the first section of the interview schedule, which measured the degree of rationalization in China's entrepreneurial class, question three ("How do you feel about China's new market economy and new societal wealth?") in particular sought to probe the minds of the entrepreneurial class and understand their feelings on the markets and wealth that have come to define contemporary China. Many of the entrepreneurs the author interviewed clearly identified with the benefits of markets and wealth. A *Baling Hou* interviewee stated the following in response to this question:

> I think this [markets and wealth in China] is what attracted a lot of *haigui* to return—because they see a lot of opportunities. They know the culture compared to foreigners who come to Shanghai to start up, and their parents are in China. The [speed of the] growth is not necessarily a good thing. For the US or Europe, the development takes over 100 years, but China is trying to do that in 10 or 20 years. For KFC, for example, they want the chicken to grow fast; but you can't obey the natural law in order to get this much chicken. So they have to put something in the chicken to make it grow. So I would say that is exactly what is happening in China. What I think is missing for the back of China's growth is a revolutionary creativity. Because it is growing relatively well, it can purchase technologies from other countries; but by doing that you are not encouraging your own technology to grow . . . this then can be a problem in the future. China is trying to get away from having this image of being the world's factory. By doing that it is encouraging creation or technology development (Entrepreneur 7).

In late 2010, *China Daily* reported on a young woman, and now entrepreneur, who capitalized on China's newfound economic organization and the opportunities that it increasingly provides. Cao Shun was a young success in China, who at an early age elevated herself into a position at a foreign company (an office manager in a top 500 company in Shanghai) where she enjoyed a high salary (75,000 USD per year) and quality of life. This position was associated with long hours and a very stressful environment, which in her mind was not consistent with her dream. Thus, after several years in this occupation she decided to transfer her talents and efforts to the world of entrepreneurship, despite the monetary security afforded to her in this position, and established her own business in the baking industry. Though many discouraged her from this seemingly irrational idea, she applied what transformative thought and experience she had acquired through her interaction with China's markets to her newfound enterprise—and this led directly to the overwhelming prosperity of her enterprise (Wang Yan, 2010).

The majority of entrepreneurs' responses to the first section of questions were rational in nature: they identified a stark difference between their parents' generation and the post-reform generations, as well as the specific opportunities and wealth now available to them, and their desire to take advantage of this newfound environment. One particular entrepreneur had recently moved from a white-collar well-paid position with Hyundai and Sino Consulting in order to begin his own consulting firm. At the time of the interview, he had already indicated a high level of success in his venture. This move alone—from the white-collar private sector to his creation of a consulting firm—indicated his rationality and autonomy in shifting his focus toward the opportunities that are growing within the opening of the economy. In the interview he stated that "he wants to enlarge his company, to make the company bigger for the future . . . since they want to enlarge the company as much as possible, they also want to make the system better in order to realize this outcome" (Entrepreneur 1). As he revealed later in the interview, his comment on the "system's improvement" is in reference to the ongoing issues that Chinese entrepreneurs face in terms of property and the rule of law, specifically related to issues of taxation as well as a legal system that fails to protect private property (discussed in detail in the following chapter). In response to the question "As a result of China's modernization, do you feel that a new mentality has emerged in China's entrepreneurs?," he stated: "In the old times when they had a certain income they were content with this fixed amount; but now they are not happy with the status quo. They want to keep pace with the development, and they are open and see the ways that other countries have prospered and want to maximize on opportunities" (Entrepreneur 1).

One of the longer and more liberal interview experiences occurred with a Beijing entrepreneur, who began his own enterprise about ten years ago after leaving employment at a State-Owned Enterprise (SOE). His enterprise represents US construction material manufacturers in China attempting to introduce their products and technology to the Chinese markets. In response to the question "How do you feel about China's new market economy and societal wealth?" he stated the following:

> People like money and they like to live a better life; they like to enjoy the benefits of wealth. I think most Chinese are still in the stage of getting money, but they don't know yet how to enjoy the money. I think the second generation after me will be able to enjoy the actual wealth that is coming to China, maybe 20 to 30 years from now. . . . Right now the society is changing quickly, so everyone wants to find a better place in society. Everyone has opportunities to get money, and if they can find the right position then they can change their position in society—even a small chance could change the position of a person. For example, like us, if we could find a big project tomorrow we could win a million dollars—that is possible and in fact everything is possible in China right

> now. It is like the gold rush in China right now—everybody finds chances. My company is no different: we try to find the right products, represent them here, introduce new materials and technologies; when we find the right chances—like the Birds Nest—we will be rich tomorrow (Entrepreneur 5).

And in response to the following question—"As a result of China's modernization, do you feel that a new mentality has emerged in China's entrepreneurs?" he proceeded to say:

> I think it takes time. Right now society is changing so quickly. When the entrepreneurs own something they will begin to think differently. Right now many people in the middle class are not stable, but when they are stable and gain enough money then they can begin to do something, to think at the next level. Right now they are still rushing, trying to get more money, but they are not yet stable. For example, next time they invest in a project, maybe they lose that money; today I am poor, the next day I am rich, but the next day I could be poor. I think after sometime, maybe 10 to 20 years, after society has become stable, then people will begin to think in a different way (Entrepreneur 5).

In one particular interview with a *Baling Hou* entrepreneur the author asked "How do you feel about China's New Market Economy and Societal Wealth?" In his response, he connected what would be a frequent (liberal-oriented) response highlighting the impact that China's economic freedom is having on the evolving mentality of entrepreneurs: the economic freedom and wealth in China is positive, and it is encouraging the entrepreneurs to think past a purely economic mentality of getting rich:

> I think in China things are not balanced. You can work and have nothing and then you have a chance and can have money, it is like a gamble. I ask why are the rich very rich and the poor very poor? If you have an apartment in Shanghai 10 years ago, you can now be rich because 10 years ago the apartment is a low price, but if you don't have an apartment you cannot afford an apartment now. Is it good or bad? It is good, you have this chance to make money. Now you can realize your dream and your dream can come true. After you earn money and realize a greater quality of life your mind will change, your way of thinking about all of China (Entrepreneur 9).

When then asked "As a result of China's modernization, do you feel that a new mentality has emerged in China's entrepreneurs?," he pointed to this observable shift in the mentality of the contemporary Chinese entrepreneur compared to past generations of entrepreneurs. As he responded:

> Of course there are changes. For my parents' generation everything is different, even their way of thinking, the education and ideology was also different. The thing the previous businessmen cared about was how to earn money; the things

> I care about now are not only the money but also how I can develop my business and make it prosper. For example, if you give me a choice now of course everyone wants to get money; in this business environment you can get a lot of money nowadays. But instead of getting rich fast, I want to develop my business and take the long-term approach (even if it is less profit in the short term). The biggest difference is that before people were doing business just to get themselves food and clothes, to make themselves fat, and that is why they only care about money. But now they are not just fat and have clothes but they also have a house and other things, so now they are thinking further—about development (Entrepreneur 9).

The author was able to conduct multiple interviews with several entrepreneurs over a period of one to two years, which allowed the author to observe their personal evolution and business development, and to revisit certain issues. The author had the opportunity to revisit the entrepreneur who owns the Western style restaurant in one of China's largest cities (Entrepreneur 9). In the meeting, the author asked him how his business was doing, specifically, in relation to the frustrations he previously expressed in attempting to open a second restaurant. He said that he had found an alternate location that was approved by the government, but this did not seem to ease his sense of urgency or anxiety. As he explained, he must move quickly to expand his restaurant, not only with a second one but ideally a number of additional locations, since in China, where the act of copying proven ideas is pervasive, there is no guarantee that his successful business model will remain protected. In his opinion, his only recourse is to expand in quantity and quality in order to establish an exclusive identity for his enterprise.

As the author was concluding an interview in the spring of 2012, the particular entrepreneur stated: "The main reason why I created my company is to create freedom for myself" (Entrepreneur 18). This reflects the emerging mentality of China's emerging entrepreneurial class: they recognize the opportunities available to them as a result of significant economic reforms, and they have sought to capitalize on them pursue individual interests, respond to market demands, and secure wealth. The evolution of a rational entrepreneurial class has been a significant social consequence of the shift in economic policy beginning in 1978. The continuation of capitalist development in China should not only continue to fuel the growth of an increasingly rational entrepreneurial class, but also one that exercises a new mentality: one of independent thought and one that shatters the former mystical perception of, and absolute devotion to, the political authority and its ideology. This secularization and autonomization of the entrepreneurial class is the focus of the following section.

THE AUTONOMIZATION AND SECULARIZATION OF THE ENTREPRENEUR

The reforms Deng Xiaoping spearheaded in 1978 were significant in that they represented an unprecedented move in China toward market reforms, sanctioned by the party, and that they stood in stark ideological contrast to the party's foundation of Marxism-Leninism and Mao Zedong Thought. These reforms have benefited the party by making China richer and improving quality of life; but they have also created problems of legitimacy including the erosion of its ideological foundation (Shi Jiangtao, 2012). As a recent media piece reports:

> Deng's 1992 trip virtually saved the party as well as Deng because the credibility of one-party rule had been at stake since the 1989 crackdown. . . . But Deng's southern tour had its limits. It focused mainly on economic problems in an attempt to break away from Marxist dogmatism, but made no mention of political change. It did nothing to restart political and cultural developments that stalled after Tiananmen . . . to many analysts, the lack of substantial political reform has induced major political, cultural and moral regression on the mainland over the past two decades. Beijing's all-out pursuit of high growth has not filled the void left by the bankrupted communist ideology, and neither have efforts to revive traditional Confucian values (Shi Jiangtao, 2012).

Hu Jintao's ideological campaign was one indication that the CCP has implicitly acknowledged its declining ability to manage the social products of modernization, and is thus increasingly scrambling to legitimize its authority through the socialist mechanism of ideological rectification. In Hu Jintao's excerpt in the party's ideological periodical, *Qiu Shi*, he states "we must be fully aware that international hostile forces are stepping up efforts to implement their strategies of westernizing and dividing China, with ideology and culture being key areas of their long-term infiltration. We need to be thoroughly aware of the seriousness and complexity of the struggle in the ideological field" (Hu Jintao, 2012). Furthermore, Hu Jintao and the political elite decided to reassert the party's ideological indoctrination over social forces by carrying out campaigns reminiscent of the Maoist era (WSJ, 2012a, 9). As one article notes:

> Beijing is turning up the Cultural Revolution rhetoric in Hong Kong again. In recent months, state-owned media and Chinese officials vilified a businessman for donating money to opposition politicians, labeling them American stooges. They then threatened to expel the U.S. consul general for allegedly interfering in local politics. Even the local head of the Catholic Church was blasted as a "political mercenary" (WSJ, 2012a, 9).

The party has also promoted an ideological campaign, based on the example of Lei Feng, to persuade citizens to express greater loyalty to the party. As one Hong Kong media report said, the Chinese people need to emulate Lei Feng and his purported example and calling to be loyal to the state and to uphold socialism (Zhai, 2012). Indeed, the party's ideological campaign to continue a long-standing method of ideological rectification—to disseminate the legacy of Lei Feng throughout society—is a direct response to the growth of societal unrest related to dissatisfaction with the party.

The party's emphasis on, and utilization of, Lei Feng is symbolic of a long-standing approach, that of employing ideological rectification campaigns, through educational institutions, media outlets, and official messaging, in order to indoctrinate societal actors (Zhai, 2012). Historically, this has proved effective in the absence of economic freedoms and their marked effect of liberating minds from the shackles of the party's purported truths; thus the push for governmental accountability, checks and balances, legal institutionalization, and the like, was successfully circumvented. However, in contemporary China, the effect of economic freedom in liberating minds and creating secularized and autonomous social elements, particularly among the entrepreneurial class, is rendering indoctrination campaigns far less effective.

A *South China Morning Post* article detailed the history of Lei Feng and how the party has used this story to push large-scale indoctrination campaigns in support of the party's authority and monopoly on political power. The party has invoked Lei Feng on numerous occasions since 1978, beginning in the 1980s after the party began to see the social consequences of its newfound economic reform policies. More recently, the party once again invoked Lei Feng: the party said it would "promote the spirit of Lei Feng in companies, schools, communities, villages and online." This campaign focused on promoting Lei Feng's "unconditional love for the party." The article also quoted a Beijing-based philosopher who said "Lei wasn't a citizen but a screw in the giant party machine" and that "the leaders want everyone to be like Lei Feng, a pure collectivist who doesn't care about individual freedom and personal interests" (Zhai, 2012).

The party's strategy in using Lei Feng to indoctrinate society is a typical case of its exercise of ideological engineering in order to engender social passivity and support, while the issue of Lei Feng also highlights the nature of China's educational system and its attempts to control ideas from an early age. For example, according to the same *South China Morning Post* article, schools would receive special guests, such as Lu Jinhua, who was the architect of the "Lei Feng diary campaign" decades ago, and Lu would expound on the purported virtues of Lei Feng. Yet, one member of the camera crew was quoted as saying "I'm so sick of these [tributes]" which he also said "are so fake." This sentiment is not uncommon among Chinese citizens today, and many are skeptical of the portrait the party paints of him, and some even of his existence (Zhai, 2012).

The author's interviews with members of China's entrepreneurial class, and analysis of contemporary news media reports and research reports within China, reveals an entrepreneurial class that is breaking with official state ideology and beginning to think independently. One particular entrepreneur, who resides and works in one of China's largest cities, explicated on the vastness and unique nature of China's growth, pointing to the clear break that has taken shape between pre- and post-reform environments as a result of markets and wealth, which has forced the emerging entrepreneurial generation to learn on their own:

> It is very fast. It is an overwhelming revolution; it changes our minds. But people in my generation cannot gain any life experience from their parents, because their parents didn't experience such a big change. So they have to learn everything on their own; they have to find their own way . . . so for your question I think the change, it is a good change, growing always (Entrepreneur 10).

When asked "how does your life differ from your parents?" one particular entrepreneur said it's less "manufactured." As she elaborated:

> For their generation they have ways of thinking in life, specifically a more manufactured way of thinking. So many things are the same for that generation, their paths are the same. My parents are somewhat of an anomaly, since my mom opened her business when I was really young. But most other people from that generation will have very similar experiences. Not meaning for occupation or anything, but they will experience the same things such as natural disasters and the Cultural Revolution. Many people graduated without work so the government encouraged them to do labor in countryside. But for my generation we call ourselves *Baling Hou* (born after 1980). This generation is a little different, because China opened its gate right at our generation. My parents' generations will be the first to experience this as an adult. For us we are losing what we had before very quickly. For their generation nothing changed, for ages really. But for us, within 10 years many buildings are gone, and for our childhood maybe we cannot see that again; that is why is it so special for the "*Baling Hou*" age. And I think that won't appear again for a long time in China's history (Entrepreneur 7).

One particular Beijing-based entrepreneur indicated his capacity to understand not only the opportunities that markets now present in China but also the autonomy that naturally stems from this opportunity: "My life is very different from my parents' life. Freedom . . . now I can bring freedom into play, and I can exercise individual ability and competence and without the overarching control that previously existed" (Entrepreneur 13).

An interview with a female entrepreneur in one of China's larger coastal cities revealed the liberal nature of Chinese entrepreneurship and China's emergent entrepreneurial class. Although now an entrepreneur in the coastal area, she was born and spent much of her youth in China's interior, an economic area and social community that has remained relatively underdeveloped. She explained that the people in her hometown still adhere to traditional customs and norms in areas such as marriage and work, and leisure activities, including perceptions of entrepreneurship (Entrepreneur 15). For example, her parents' concern and opposition to her decision to relocate to the coast were related to the risk involved in embarking upon the occupation of entrepreneurship, as well as cultural issues such as delaying marriage in pursuit of socioeconomic gain and independence. In generalizing the landscape in her hometown, she stated that people avoid taking risks and instead work in any job that provides security; and outside of the working world most do the same traditional and limited activities—such as mahjong. They fail to embody an independent mentality. Indeed, even though her friends have attempted to bring their model of entrepreneurship to her hometown, it has thus far been rejected due to the "introverted" mentality of the people in that area (Entrepreneur 15).

As she explained, the environment of economic freedom, and the opportunity for entrepreneurship, in conjunction with the younger generation and the rise in Internet mediums for discussion and idea sharing, is eroding the traditional conception of an absolute state ideology and a singular social mentality—factors which should have an impact on the future development of her hometown. As she noted:

> The Chinese education is one that enforces absolute truth, not encouraging independent thought. But the younger generations are breaking away from this and thinking independently. In China you have to show a respect—a weird respect—for older generations. Education is always one-way, no exchange of ideas. One of my friends who is a teacher at a school wanted to create an open environment for the kids, an innovative way to inspire the kids to learn English, not just repeat things. She said the chairman of the school rejects this idea; and says China doesn't provide this type of education. Thus the creativity and openness of the kids are still very limited. For me I had the traditional learning, but I am more open, not mainstream. This has a lot to do with the Internet, entrepreneurship and discussions with other people (Entrepreneur 15).

This particular entrepreneur rejected the cultural paradigm in which she grew up, despite the lack of support she faced within her own community, both from her family and the general environment, and instead, embraced China's newfound sphere of economic freedom. Thus, she reflects both economic rationality and autonomous thought: she enjoys museums and galleries in her spare time, which in her words, is representative of a newfound philosophy characterized by independent thought and pursuit, contrasted with adherence to the robotic life she describes in the less developed areas including her hometown; and she pursues an entrepreneurship that not only attempts to develop a successful business model, but furthermore, one that is equally intentional about developing a sense of social responsibility (Entrepreneur 15).

One particular entrepreneur indicated the strength of this growing rationality and autonomy among China's contemporary entrepreneurs during an interview with the author in 2011. Her comments reflected a thorough understanding of China's socioeconomic and political growth as well as the host of problems that have emerged related to the lack of the rule of law and the continuation of a one-party system. She expressed a deep concern over the growing volatility as a result of these unaddressed issues, yet also expressed hope for China because of the continued growth of this class (Entrepreneur 14). This was a common theme throughout the author's interviews: entrepreneurs expressed concern over these institutional issues in China, yet at the same time carried a degree of optimism about China's future, an optimism that derived from the growth of this new entrepreneurial class in China.

At the end of an interview with Entrepreneur 14, she asked: can I talk more about China's danger? Pleased to hear her desire to continue our discussion, she proceeded to state the following:

> Pay attention to farmers that lost their land. They are easily fooled because they are not educated, and so the government used very cheap money to steal their land and told them "I'll give you free apartments," etc. "and you can go to cities to work and make more money." So they were excited to come to Shanghai, Beijing etc., and make money. But their kids?: No insurance, schools, jobs etc. And the numbers are huge—about 1/3 of the people in China. That is why they don't allow a belief system in China—it worries the regime; it is an excuse to control this group of people. If there is a belief system, and people start to fear natural things, then maybe things can change (Entrepreneur 14).

A final example will help illustrate the growing secularization of the entrepreneur. An interview in 2012 revealed just how different the emerging entrepreneurs are from the other groups inside China. First of all, this particular entrepreneur was the creator of the mobile app described above—a creation that reflected significant independent thought and initiative, not only in its design but also in its objective of targeting a specific group in demand.

Furthermore, she spoke at length on how the entrepreneurial class is uniquely placed within China's opening up. They reflect the highest level of independent and individual thought; they are innovators, problem solvers, and as she would later note, (political) troublemakers. As a result, the party is increasingly worried over this very development (Entrepreneur 17):

> Products change the world. I was in a third tier city and on the radio they were talking about concepts such as innovation, solving problems, the buzz words, etc. The Chinese government didn't want this. We were not raised to solve problems—in our education. Our education has killed the ability to identify and solve problems. Really I think the political system doesn't want any trouble, and the government is fearful of independent thinking college students. So we get this kind of rigorous training, but it's all based on memorization. The most important skill is first to identify the problem before solving the problem. I work with seemingly creative people, but it has shocked me how uncreative they are; and it is very challenging for them to solve problems because they can't identify them in the first place (these are designers, programmers, etc—and they are quite typical) (Entrepreneur 17).

The advent of economic freedom and the diffusion of markets has created a rational entrepreneurial class clinching the increasing opportunities available in growing markets and a class conscious of the state's former and current attempts to undermine independent thought and determine the political values of its citizenry, through an ideological framework that justifies one-party domination. This emerging capitalist class has indicated an opposition to this intentional limitation on societal thought. This opposition by the entrepreneurial class is derived from its recognition of the restrictions this places on the health of the economic sphere in general and the economic values of the entrepreneurs in particular, such as, an independent, innovative, and industrious spirit. This rationalization and secularization of the entrepreneur, which in the Western transition symbolized the first blow to the political institutions in creating a foundation based upon independence and initiative, was imperative for the eventual evolution of a bourgeoisie: it set the stage for a decisive philosophical victory, which would evolve into specific interests, and eventually a demand for certain rights, namely property rights and protections.

CONCLUSION

China's decision to reform its economic policy and open up to the world in 1978 was significant; but the decision by Deng Xiaoping in 1993 following his southern tour to accelerate capitalist development and its consequence—development of markets and the rise of private enterprises and private entrepreneurs—was even more profound: it represented a clear break in an over decade-long intra-party battle between hardliners and reformers over the move to implement new and unprecedented economic policy. The wide array of opportunities now available in China through the proliferation of markets has necessarily created the impetus for the rise of social elements to fill these growing demands, motivated by the potential returns on their investments and production activities. The markets that entrepreneurs have targeted are diverse, and reflective of the growth of capitalism and the evolving characteristics of the Chinese entrepreneur: mobile technology innovation and development (Entrepreneur 17); products and services that support a safe food supply and improve food quality, and combat growing issues within the food industry stemming from the lack of the rule of law (Entrepreneur 18); and the creation of business incubators that seek to mobilize this entrepreneurial spirit and assist it in business development (Entrepreneur 7), and in meeting the demands of emerging markets in China. Thus, the entrepreneur has become a rational actor with a drive to locate and secure opportunities, to innovate and transcend former achievements in product development and business design, and to create wealth.

China's entrepreneurs, as a result of the growth in markets and the rise of a rational mentality, have also become increasingly autonomous. Entrepreneurs recognize the lack of autonomy, and conformance to state-sponsored ideologies, which characterized previous generations, and have moved away from this mode and mentality: they support and value autonomy, including individual thought and economic initiative, and understand its importance in promoting economic growth and quality of life. As a result, the party is faced with a much more difficult task in its quest to manufacture a politically benign and dependent society. Most importantly, the rationality and autonomy that defines this emergent class demonstrates an evolution through stage one of the three-stage growth that characterizes liberalism. The following chapter will explore the extent to which they have progressed through stage two, and by doing so have developed defined legal interests purposed with protecting private property and the overall economic environment within which they operate.

Chapter Five

China's Private Entrepreneurs

State Predation and the Rise of Property-Law Interests

This chapter examines China's rule by law environment and the extent to which its resultant official corruption and state predation has affected China's entrepreneurs. Chinese corruption is widespread and especially pervasive at the local level, despite successive attempts by China's leaders to curb this phenomenon and enlarging trend. The latest—Xi Jinping's anti-corruption drive—has sought to make significant progress in stamping out corruption. Yet, Xi's campaign appears to be purposed with targeting and purging potential political opposition more than actually combating corruption. Indeed, China's corruption remains widespread according to independent assessments, despite Xi's attempts. This has the likely effect of alienating China's private entrepreneurial class, whose existence centers on property protection, and providing the impetus for the rise of property-law interests among this class. Thus, this chapter seeks to answer the following research questions: What is the nature of corruption in contemporary China? To what extent has China's embrace of the *rule by law* exacerbated corruption and state predation, particularly as it affects the entrepreneurial class? Are China's entrepreneurs forming and advancing legal and property-law interests consistent with classical liberal values as a result of China's rule by law governance?

POLITICAL CORRUPTION AND PROPERTY RIGHTS IN CONTEMPORARY CHINA

Official Corruption and the Rule by Law in Contemporary China: an Overview

Corruption is no stranger to China. More specifically referred to as "official deviance," this illicit behavior has been defined as "all forms of behavior that deviate from the prescribed norms of a regime, in which individuals or groups exploit the formal organization instead of working for it, and in which personal roles take precedence over organizational roles" (Xiaobo Lü, 2000, 12). Historically, and certainly in the case of China, corruption has reared its pernicious head in one of three ways: graft, which involves an illicit deal or agreement with an official, such as bribes; rent-seeking, which in an economic context refers to officials who oversee crucial industries within an economy, and thus who determine the distribution of resources, allocating to those economic actors that are willing to pay up (Xiaobo Lü, 2000, 12–13); or prebendalism, which "deviates from the norms of public office—in this case the party/state—with a goal of private gain that is primarily non-economic and political in nature" (Xiaobo Lü, 2000, 13). In Xiaobo Lü's view, in terms of corruption, the paramount problem for the party today is "between the state and its agencies and agents utilizing state authority to achieve ends that ultimately serve their private interests" (2000, 251), at the center of which are China's rising private entrepreneurs.

The end of socialist revolution and the rise of free markets and economic freedom have complicated the issue of corruption for the party; indeed, the party's attempts to modernize and reform the polity have not only modified the nature of corruption, but have likely exacerbated many of its forms (Xiaobo Lü, 2000, 235). As McGregor writes "only one thing has altered dramatically over time—the size of bribes, which now routinely run into the millions of dollars, even for relatively low-level officials" (McGregor, 2010, 139). From 1949 to the end of Mao's reign, China pursued the "politicization . . . of the bureaucracy" to achieve "continuous revolution" (Xiaobo Lü, 2000, 230–231), which included only a brief embrace of the Soviet model of bureaucracy before returning to Mao's signature mass line, as well as the "elevations and expansion of the power of the party in administrative affairs" (Xiaobo Lu, 2000, 75; 74–75) which failed to create organizational and institutional integrity, and fueled—instead of eliminated—various forms of corruption. In post-Mao China, a different strategy has been embraced, that is, the "depoliticization of the bureaucracy" to achieve "modernization" (Xiaobo Lü, 2000, 230–231). But here again, results have fallen far short of expectations. Despite modernization attempts, including the expansion of laws and rules and norms, corruption continues unabated, and remains a significant threat to the stability and legitimacy of the party (Xiaobo Lü, 2000, 231–232).

China's drive to craft a functioning bureaucracy has created a host of rules, laws, and institutions in appearance only instead of substantive legal reform and enforcement, and its production of even more laws and rules will continue to prove futile until legal institutionalization, or the rule of law, is implemented. The central government's slow loss of power over localities, and localities' growing power and autonomy, highlight this problem. Similar to other communist regimes, China has created rules and laws, and anti-corruption institutions, yet these institutions are either restricted in who they can target (discussed further below), disregarded entirely by officials, or simply co-opted by them, especially at the local levels, in that they place friendly personage in key positions. Moreover, officials not only abuse their regulatory power, which fuels informal relations between state agencies and society in general, but also use their (unchecked) power to benefit family and friends (Xiaobo Lü, 2000, 240–254). The result: "equipped with regulatory power, but without effective institutional constraints, state agencies have tapped into the new opportunities to seek profits from the rapidly growing number of businesses and other profit or non-profit organizations" (Xiaobo Lü, 2000, 252).

As mentioned above, the party's tacit allowance of corruption can be seen in a protective mechanism built into the vertical superstructure of the party organization that acts to protect officials who engage in corruption. Firstly, party officials accused of corruption are not accessible for investigation by non-party authorities, in other words, they can only be investigated "in-house" so to speak by the party inspection organ—the Central Commission for Discipline Inspection in Beijing. Secondly, even this commission is limited in its ability to investigate: before moving forward with an investigation, it must first find approval from the party body above the official who is suspected; thus in effect, it becomes very difficult to prosecute official corruption—especially corruption at the highest levels. If a Politburo Standing Committee member, for example, who sits on the highest body in China, were to be investigated, the Commission would be required to seek the blessings of the leader of China in order to move forward (McGregor, 2010, 137–140).

To be sure, China has attempted to curb corruption through the implementation of a number of institutional reforms, similar to those efforts to implement political institutional reforms in the 1980s and 1990s by Deng Xiaoping and Jiang Zemin (see Jing Huang, 2008), though with much less success. In particular, beginning in the 1990s, China moved to improve the integrity of existing anticorruption statutes as well as to implement new anticorruption measures. The most salient reforms to existing laws include the following: whereas previously officials charged with corruption were not burdened with providing proof that their income was legitimate, with these reforms officials were required to demonstrate that their incomes were obtained legally; whereas previously those who presented bribes were not the focus of attention (the receivers of these bribes were the primary focus), with these reforms the state increased the severity of penalties for those initiating bribes, which included life in prison; the death sentence was introduced for senior officials who had engaged in corruption; beginning in 2001 party officials posted at the ministry level or higher were included in audits when stepping down from their posts; abolishing the use of fake names when establishing financial accounts; and holding senior officials in government organs and organizations responsible for corruption within their organization (even if they are not complicit) (Dali Yang, 2004).

New measures have also been implemented, most notably, reforms to government accounting, budgeting, and expenditures in the form of greater oversight from the center. Reforms to budgeting sought primarily to address the pervasive problem of "extra-budget" funds and accounts, which encouraged localities to issue arbitrary fees and fines on the local population. To combat this, the center required that these funds be reported in the budget and delivered to the government treasury, which shifted control of these funds from local governments to finance departments. Localities also lost a degree of control over expenditures due to corrupt management of public funds, which included the creation of and payment to "ghost payrolls." These reforms resulted in a large reduction in government payrolls and in turn curbed what previously was an enormous amount of waste. Finally, the center also imposed greater control over government accounting. Whereas budget reforms sought to eliminate arbitrary fees and fines, and expenditure reforms sought to reduce "ghost payrolls," reforms to accounting sought to reduce widespread embezzlement, particularly officials' use of public funds for personal entertainment (Dali Yang, 2004).

Xi Jinping has also ostensibly fought corruption through his anti-corruption drive, beginning in 2012. According to one account, this drive has identified some 1.5 million corrupt cadres. Yet, not surprisingly, this campaign appears to be less driven by an actual desire to root out corruption and more driven by Xi's vision to purge the party of potential opposition (Fiol-Mahon, 2018). To be sure, some of the high ranking officials that have become victims of Xi's campaign are known opponents: over a two year period "more than twenty of the forty-four officials at the vice-ministerial level or higher whom the CCDI had removed had close ties or financial connections with Zhou Yongkang, considered one of Xi's most formidable political adversaries" (Economy, 2018, 34). Moreover, Xi's anti-corruption campaign runs the risk of backfiring in that the intensity and scale of this campaign is likely to expose the pervasiveness of Chinese corruption (Economy, 2018, 33). Finally, Xi's anti-corruption campaign over the past eight years or so appears to have made little progress in reducing corruption. According to Transparency International's Corruption Perceptions Index, which measures corruption on a scale of 0–100, where 0 is "highly corrupt" and 100 is "very clean," China's rating since 2012 (39) has been very poor, and only made a slight jump—two points—when comparing its 2012 rating (39) to its 2019 (41) rating. Further, its 2014 and 2015 rating dropped 3 points and 2 points respectively, signaling a worsening state of corruption years into Xi's anti-corruption campaign (Transparency International, 2017). In short, Xi's campaign, much like previous anti-corruption drives, appears to be ineffective at actually reducing corruption and rather effective at clearing out intra-party rivals, while presenting the risk of highlighting—to an increasingly rational and secular society—China's unchecked corruption and the rule by law system that underpins its pervasiveness.

Thus, as noted above, the overall results of these reforms have been nominal (Xiaobo Lü, 2000, 254). As Dali Yang notes in his conclusion, the nefarious use of public funds by officials have only "been somewhat moderated . . . the paradox of the anti-corruption drive has been this: in recent years so many officials have been charged with corruption, and the amount of money involved in each corruption case has risen so much, that even optimists about the antigraft drive must question their own judgment about whether corruption can be tamed in China" (2004, 248). Moreover, this pervasive corruption has been specially onerous on China's private entrepreneurs and their business operations: although the state "took measures to reduce its intervention in routine operations of enterprises and to prohibit state agencies from extracting non-tax funds from the enterprises . . . so far results are limited" (Xiaobo Lü, 2000, 254). Indeed, this sentiment that corruption continues to pervade China's officialdom and inflict society with growing consequences, is echoed loudly by the entrepreneurial community, evidenced in the author's personal interviews, Chinese media, and survey results detailed below.

A Survey of Prominent Corruption Cases

This section highlights major cases of endemic corruption and the resultant outcry from society in general, and China's private entrepreneurs in particular. This includes the arrogation of property in the rural village of Wukan; Bo Xilai's reign of terror as Chongqing's Party Secretary; targeting private entrepreneurs and their property under the guise of reducing crime and corruption; the train crash in Wenzhou and the fire in Shanghai's Jing'an District; and the rise of China's "princelings."

The explosive surge in social unrest in Wukan, China, is a prime example of China's growing state-society cleavage as a result of pervasive corruption. According to media sources, this unrest was in response to "local officials who commandeer farmland at below market prices and then sell it to developers and pocket most of the profits" (Page and Spegele, 2011). The issue centered on dealings between two companies: Lufeng Fengtian Livestock

Products (owning a large pig farm in Wukan) and Country Garden (one of China's largest property developers). The owner of Lufeng Fengtian was the former Deputy Chairman of the government of Lufeng, which includes the village of Wukan. It appears the intent was for Lufeng Fengtian to sell not only personal property but also the property of other villagers to the property developer, while providing nominal compensation to the villagers, and therefore generating high profits from the deal. As the article notes, "villagers in Wukan have accused local officials of selling farmland to a property developer for as much as one billion *yuan* ($157 million), and then pocketing 70 percent of the proceeds" (Page and Spegele, 2011). This piqued the victims of this property theft, causing one of the largest occurrences of social unrest in contemporary China, and reflects the increasing proliferation of official graft in China, especially at the local levels, for aforementioned reasons (Ljunggren, 2012; Spegele, 2012b).

Indeed, this case spans even further than the plight of China's farmers in Wukan; it also involved an important intra-party factional battle—between Chongqing Party Chief Bo Xilai and Guangdong Party Chief Wang Yang—that garnered significant media coverage in the months leading up to China's important leadership transition, as a result of these leaders' contrasting political views: Bo Xilai a nostalgic Maoist and Wang Yang a liberal reformer. Both party officials oversaw the endemic abuse of official power, specifically targeting the private property of individuals, though each party official responded in a different fashion. In Wang Yang's prefecture, which includes the farmers in Wukan, the Party Chief was instrumental in supporting the people's requests for curbing official corruption and implementing measures for property right's protection, as well as in supporting the growth of a civil society (Page, 2012d). In contrast, in Bo Xilai's prefecture, allegations have surfaced that officials abused their political power and that local officials arbitrarily seized entrepreneurs' property in the name of cracking down on "organized crime" (Page, 2012c). Indeed, affected entrepreneurs "alleged that they were accused of being gangsters so that their assets could be expropriated" (WSJ, 2012b). One business owner, Zhang Mingyu, took to social media and "hinted that he had fresh details about the Wang Lijun case," and then disappeared in early March (Page, 2012b, 4). Meanwhile, Bo Xilai's praises from party leaders and expectations for elevation within the party witnessed a sudden halt with his demotion from his prominent position on 15 March (Page, 2012e).

This case exemplifies the pervasiveness of China's official usurpation—in this case exercising both extortion and abuse of police powers. Some of the entrepreneurs affected by Bo and his tactics have spoken out, one of which was arbitrarily detained and beaten (WSJ, 2012b). Media reports have revealed some of the businessmen that were targeted in Bo Xilai's campaign, though as commonly understood in China, the information that is allowed to leak out only represents the tip of the iceberg. Two of the entrepreneurial victims include Li Jun and Zhang Mingyu: "Li Jun, a businessman who lost his $700 million company . . . says he was tortured by the police and military for three months for a false confession" (WSJ, 2012b); and Zhang Mingyu said he was seized by authorities and forced to remain in a "guest house" until Bo Xilai was removed from office (Choi Chi-yuk, 2012b).

The high-speed train crash in Wenzhou, derailing two trains, killing 40 people and injuring nearly 200 (BBC News, 2011), and the 2010 fire in Shanghai's Jing'an district, burning a high rise building and killing 53, highlight another aspect of endemic Chinese corruption (BBC News, 2010). Both cases represent a common problem: officials in various state agencies, as a result of their regulatory powers and control over resources, accept bribes and engage in profiteering at the expense of construction safety and construction standards. In the recent high-speed train crash in China's southern area of Wenzhou—a case of abuse of powers associated with the control of resources and regulation—the Chinese leadership has indicated that corruption was at the heart of this incident (Tien, 2012). A media piece reported that China's State Council said that "top Railway Ministry officials" are responsible for the crash, particularly, for their lack of regulation and for allowing "poorly designed track-signal equipment" and "inadequate safety procedures" (Areddy, 2011, 3).

Reports inside China indicate that corruption associated with railway construction is not isolated to Wenzhou. According to one report, the former deputy chief engineer at the Ministry of Railways, Zhang Shuguang, and close advisor to former railways minister Liu Zhijun, were both indicated in not only taking 1 billion RMB in bribes, but furthermore, in stealing 187 million RMB from a high speed rail project. The implications of the missing 187 million RMB are significant: 187 million RMB were withheld from railway projects, thus filling the pockets of corrupt officials instead of ensuring the integrity of the rail system. As in many cases, this was only the tip of the iceberg. It appears Su Shuhu, another high-ranking official with the Ministry of Railways, is also suspected of similar corruption (Jiao, 2011).

The fire that engulfed a 28-story high-rise residential building in the Jing'an district of Shanghai is yet another example of the consequences of China's endemic corruption. In this particular case, the building was in need of structural repairs, which were overseen by local authorities in Jing'an. According to the accounting of events leading up to the fire, the work was contracted out to a Shanghai based company (Shanghai Jiayi Decoration Company) that had managed to bribe its way into winning the contract. Furthermore, as part of the bribes, safety authorities exercised a hands-off approach, allowing the decoration company to conduct unsupervised structural repairs. In the process of welding, the underqualified, inexperienced crew managed to set fire to insulation that spread to the bamboo scaffolding, eventually setting fire to the entire high-rise structure (Yu Ran, 2011). One of China's rising legal figures, Yuan Yulai, in support of constitutional governance and those individuals who fall victim to state predation, attempted to provide legal aid to 21 of the victims in this tragic incident. He requested that the municipal government "release details about the distribution of donations, [the] list of [members of the] work committee assigned to the fire [investigation] and documents showing that the apartment building had passed previous fire-safety tests" (Yan, 2012), but the locality simply denied his request.

Local agencies and officials aren't the only ones benefiting from unchecked powers; a prominent—and proliferating—problem is a variety of immunities for elites and their princelings. As Yiyi Lu states, daily media reports out of China reveal the frequency of these abuses: the mayor of Hubei Province runs a red light and hits a 14-year old student, but is allowed to continue with routine business; and an official from Henan Province reprimands and threatens a policeman after being pulled over for fake tags (Yiyi Lu, 2011). Elites also control key economic resources at will. As one article notes, "The state owns all urban land and strategic industries, as well as banks, which dole out loans overwhelmingly to state-run companies. The big spoils thus go to political insiders who can leverage political connections and family prestige to secure resources and then mobilize the same networks to protect them" (Page, 2011). Indeed, the author's interview with an entrepreneur in early 2012 illuminated this issue, that is, of leaders placing family members, especially children, in key industries of the economy—and the consequence of this for the entrepreneurial class. As he said:

> Parents who are business owners tell their kids to go into government; and parents who are in government tell their kids to go into business. As an official you have a good life—people invite you for a lot of dinners, you have respect; but no money. You have power, and the money comes from the business people. The government official thus always thinks I want my kid to be in business; I have power and connections, and so I can help my kids to do business—combine wealth and power. People in business on the other hand, feel, every day I have to beg officials for help, to provide dinner and gifts for them, give them money, etc. (Entrepreneur 16).

This is especially important in the fact that many are concerned over the role of the princelings and their impact on China's leadership transitions, particularly in the perception that this privileged group will further entrench their elite status and subsequent control over economic resources at the expense of private enterprises and private entrepreneurs (Chang, 2012).

In the reform era, the party has retained control of key industries, not only to prevent power from transferring into the hands of an independent social base, but also to retain economic spoils for the leadership and their families. One particular entrepreneur, with whom the author interviewed in the spring of 2012, elaborated on this very issue, expressing his frustration over this privileged system, the harm it brings to entrepreneurship, and its ultimate source: the one-party system. As he noted: "We want to fix these bugs stemming from the government: Wen Jiabao's son controls the satellite company; the former vice-premier's daughter, Mrs. Li, controls China electricity, and leadership families' control of China's tobacco groups, to name a few" (Entrepreneur 18).

China's endemic corruption, especially among local agencies and officials, is a problem China's leadership knows it must get under its control. The consequence of this (unchecked) regulatory power in the hands of local agencies and officials overseeing an economy in transition is growing social cleavage, disaffection and even opposition to the party. Most notable is the growing frustration within the emerging entrepreneurial community, evidenced in the literature and in the author's personal discussions with this enterprising class. The following section seeks to assess the entrepreneurial class's perceptions of corruption and the extent to which they are developing property-law interests in response.

THE RISE OF ENTREPRENEURS' PROPERTY-LAW INTERESTS

The nature of China's current political system and political regime—a single-party authoritarian state—and what it has sanctioned if not at times greatly encouraged since 1978—an economic environment within which actors are free to choose the details of their respective economic lives and to possess and amass property and wealth, has led to a fundamental and growing contradiction between state and society. As the foregoing discussion in this chapter has indicated, the levels and pervasiveness of corruption in China is something that plagues most people from farmers in the countryside to entrepreneurs in China's symbol of modernization—the city of Shanghai. Thus, an important question is: how are China's entrepreneurs reacting and responding to the current lack of legal protections, particularly protections on private property, which seeks to threaten their very livelihood, and in turn the greater prosperity of the nation as a whole? Are they indifferent? If not are they responding in ways analogous to the early British commercial community, or even the

Chinese commercial and gentry classes, that is, by drawing near to the state in order to secure privileges and fiscal-legal immunities? Or is the object of their interests the institutionalization of the *rule of law*?

ENTREPRENEURS CLASH WITH A PREDATORY STATE: TAXATION, THE "SAN LUAN," AND EXPROPRIATION OF PRIVATE PROPERTY

The party's monopoly over resources and regulatory powers, as well as its overall superior politico-legal power relative to society, have created a host of problems for China's private entrepreneurs, most notably grievances related to taxation, extra-legal impositions such as the "*san luan*," expropriation of private property, and restricted access to loans. According to an article in *China Economic Times*, entrepreneurs are facing prohibitive taxation, especially as it pertains to their enterprise development, a point conveyed by private entrepreneur Liu Hanyuan at the annual National People's Congress (NPC) and Chinese People's Political Consultative Conference (CPPCC) meeting. Indeed, an investigation report on enterprise burdens nationwide found that taxation is a major burden. The report also found that 74 percent of enterprises believe the burden of taxation is "relatively heavy" and that it is an issue that needs to be immediately addressed, and 83 percent of enterprises said tax mitigation is of "chief importance." Liu Hanyuan conveyed a similar message, including that the state should continue to transform government functions, which includes rationalizing functions of power, and reducing—if not eliminating—the obstructions or restrictions that influence private enterprise development (2014).

Prohibitive taxation is only part of the overall picture. Three particular practices, due to their pervasiveness, have been coined the *san luan* or the "three unruly actions" of "illicitly levying fines," "imposing fees," and "apportioning forced donations" (Xiaobo Lü, 2000, 208), and have become a particular problem for China's entrepreneurs. Survey data revealed the following annual enterprise expenditures related to *san luan*: 43,800 *yuan* for various kinds of [forced] contributions; 62,500 *yuan* for "various kinds of donations"; and 100,400 *yuan* for "various kinds of social engagements" (Zhang Houyi, 2008, 296).

This pervasive state predation has greatly affected the business and property interests of China's entrepreneurial class, and they have indicated their stark awareness of its impact on their business operations. One particular entrepreneur expressed his grievances in the following way: "The government has too much power. . . . Regulations here mean that businessmen have to do a lot of illegal things. That gives people a real sense of insecurity." Indeed, he showed profound insight when he commented that as long as the economy is doing well, the party thinks it is "doing everything right." On the contrary, in his opinion, "another revolution will come soon" if the government doesn't address these problems (Page, 2012a, 15). Moreover, a survey of China's entrepreneurs conducted in 2011 asked to what extent China's state predation exists as well as to what extent this adverse environment is affecting their business environment. Respondents overwhelmingly acknowledged the existence of high rates of corruption as well as its effects on their business environment. When asked "How would you say the level of corruption has changed over the last few years?," 32 percent of respondents answered that "it is getting much worse," 31 percent of respondents answered "it is getting somewhat worse," and only 6 percent responded that "it is getting much better" (Gamester, 2011). Furthermore, when asked "To what extent, if at all, do you think corruption is a problem that hurts business in China?," 56 percent of Beijing-based entrepreneurs, 50 percent of Guangzhou-based entrepreneurs, and 23 percent of Shanghai-based entrepreneurs responded that "it is a serious problem that makes business difficult"; and only 9 percent of Beijing-based entrepreneurs, 16 percent of Guangzhou-based entrepreneurs, and 10 percent of Shanghai-based entrepreneurs responded that "it's not much of a problem" (Gamester, 2011).

In fact, corruption has become so pervasive in China that social elements beyond the entrepreneurial class have acknowledged the gravity and consequences of unfettered corruption. Based on a survey conducted in 1998, "top managers, senior cadres, educators, and entrepreneurs [in Beijing, Shanghai and Guangzhou] ranked anticorruption as the most important measure for promoting economic development" and "according to a 1998 survey of prefecture-level officials attending the Central Party School, 65 percent of the 121 officials believed curbing corruption was the key to winning public confidence" (Dali Yang, 2004, 221).

The banking industry, which historically has acted as a critical facilitator of entrepreneurial and enterprise growth, has not only impeded entrepreneurial and enterprise growth, but furthermore, has induced corrupt brokering between entrepreneurs and officials. Thus, the entrepreneur in many cases is left with the disadvantageous position of either avoiding the path of illegality in securing finance, or, traversing down the many opportunities for illegal finance, which has proven costly both financially and eventually "legally" when the state does decide to intervene. As one report notes: "Because banks like to maintain close ties with the large enterprises, which are mostly state-owned, only about 20 per cent of small enterprises have been granted loans. It is said that virtually no businesses with fewer than 50 staff had ever been granted a bank loan" (Zhang, 2012). Furthermore, shortages in accessing finance as a result of economic fervor have facilitated the rise in bribery and official gain in granting loans. In one case, "a farmer-turned-businessman in Hebei province bribed 80 officials in 40 different financial agencies in order to obtain 286 million *yuan* in loans" (Xiaobo Lü, 2000, 196).

The case of Wu Ying, a Chinese entrepreneur who began her business at just 17, and by 29 had become one of China's richest women, and who was charged with fraud and initially received the death penalty, exemplifies not only this issue of official graft in the absence of the rule of law, but also the avenues that China's entrepreneurs are forced to resort to in the absence of financial resources: private financiers who pool money together and loan it to entrepreneurs at high interest rates. In Wu's case, she borrowed money from several individual lenders—personal friends—and who never agreed that Wu had defrauded them. Yet, she was set to receive the death penalty for her purported finance-related crime, which was later rescinded (Ng Tzewei, 2012b; BBC News, 2012). This raised questions as to the true reason for this sentence. According to one article a possible reason is that "many officials wanted Wu dead because while in detention she gave police the names of corrupt officials she had bribed" (Ng Tzewei, 2012b).

The state's control and ownership of all land resources has also become a point of great contention for China's entrepreneurs, especially in the rising frequency in which officials exercise extortion and arbitrarily seize entrepreneur's private property. In many cases, the party officialdom simply take what they want and as they wish. The case of Bai Yiben, a hardworking and ultimately successful entrepreneur who formerly worked at one of China's SOEs, demonstrates this problem: "Powerful officials linked to China's military and Communist Party decided they wanted the fruits of his labor. . . . Officials hounded Bai . . . and his two sons . . . .manufactured state's evidence, brought suit in their own courts with no pretext of objectivity, forced the men into a life on the run and ended up with everything" (Magnier, 2004). In Bai's case a major cause for his misfortune in clashing with the local authorities was the fact that he "refused to pay bribes, take local officials out for lavish dinners" (Magnier, 2004). Bai's refusal to engage these practices determined his fate. Bai's case is representative of an endemic problem, especially at the local level; other examples include entrepreneur Cao Jiguang in Shenzhen and Yang Yongru in Shanxi Province, both of whom were victims of local seizures (Magnier, 2004).

In another case, a Guangzhou court convicted former Maoming Deputy Mayor, Yang Guangliang, for accepting bribes in excess of 34 million RMB. In similar fashion, he had accepted exorbitant amounts of money in exchange for his power in reallocating land to the highest bidder, regardless of the socioeconomic expense that accompanied the deal. This included accepting "5 million yuan from an investment company for helping secure land-use rights"

(Wang, 2011). Apparently the deputy mayor's corrupt dealings involving ownership of land date as far back as 1992 (Wang, 2011).

The Chinese firm Cathay Industrial Biotech further illuminates the consequences of state predation. This particular company had successfully engineered hydrocarbons into nylon by-products for use in areas such as diabetes drugs and lubricants, and as a result of its achievements, was approached by global companies—who use these nylon products—as future customers of Cathay Industrial Biotech. Investors in China were also ready to hedge their bets with the company. Nevertheless, according to accounts of the incident, the company's factory manager stole the technology and engineering involved, began a separate company in competition with Cathay, and is now working for and backed by the Chinese government. The company has even been granted a $300 million loan from a Chinese bank, and since then, the company and its production have been granted full backing by the party, claiming it to be vital to national security. This case highlights the party's complicit involvement in commandeering private property, and the destruction that is left in its wake (Barboza, 2011).

The case involving Gao Zhisheng, a prominent Chinese lawyer who represented the very individuals who had fallen victim to the state's arbitrary seizure of private land for personal, collective or organizational gain, and who was convicted in 2006 of "inciting subversion," not only exemplifies Chinese corruption, but furthermore, his case represents a party that refuses to limit its powers of persecution. As the authors note, "A self-trained lawyer and once rising star in China's legal establishment, Gao found himself under attack after representing some of China's most vulnerable citizens—victims of illegal land grabs" (Genser and Cohen, 2012). In fact Gao was not only a representative for those victims of land-grabs, but he was a business owner himself, owning his own law firm which was taken away from him in 2005 prior to his conviction. Since his arrest the state has threatened his family and subjected him to imprisonment and torture in undisclosed locations, while refusing to allow family members to make visits. As the media piece notes, he was last seen on April 20, 2010; and although it is unknown as to his exact location, reports suggest he is currently in a prison in China's Xinjiang Province (Genser and Cohen 2012).

China's attempts to curb corruption remain fruitless as state agencies and individuals continue to exploit their regulatory powers, producing widespread organizational and individual corruption. Nonetheless, as officials become more entrenched in these political institutions and as they become more predatory toward the entrepreneurial class, the revival of an independent-minded and legally oriented entrepreneurial class with property-law interests should emerge with equal—if not greater—force. Indeed, this is the question to which this volume now turns.

China's Private Entrepreneurs Articulate the Need for the Rule of Law

The author's interviews with entrepreneurs, as well as surveys and data analyzed in news media and research reports, show an entrepreneurial class articulating the importance of the rule of law in response to growing state predation, and in many cases over other avenues (where certain privileges or immunities are potentially obtained) such as cultivating *guanxi* or joining the party (see chapter 6).

A *Guangzhou Evening News* article reported on what are known as *yuanjiacuo'an*, or the mishandling of legal cases where people are falsely accused and unjustly charged, which have become a major problem, a problem that has obstructed the operations and development of the private sector and the businesses and entrepreneurs which operate within this sphere. NPC representative and prosecutor Zheng Hong spoke to a reporter about the state of private enterprises and private entrepreneurs and the legal changes that need to take place to provide the necessary support for this sector, saying that the Guangdong Prosecutor's office should "protect all areas of the private sector; make greater efforts to improve the way it handles legal cases; resolutely avoid obstructing business production and operations due to inappropriate handling of legal cases; and ultimately, avoid the collapse of businesses as a result of this mismanagement." He also said that the prosecutor's office should focus more on leveraging legal means to reduce corruption, especially corruption that impedes and erodes private business operations, and "diligently focus on its most critical areas, particularly the equal protection of medium and small enterprises" (Dong Liu, 2016).

Chinese media outlet *China Economic Times* explained that China's entrepreneurial class in general, and their attempts to create and develop enterprises in particular, are experiencing formidable obstacles, founded in China's severe lack of legal institutionalization, which has caused a feeling of extreme anxiety among entrepreneurs when attempting to "earn money." Zhuang Congsheng, member of the All-China Federation of Industry and Commerce, stated that "personal property that is not adequately protected" has become "the greatest cause for worry among China's private entrepreneurial class." As one Chinese attorney explained, China's courts are all-powerful, and in a matter of seconds can take your wealth, your capital, or your enterprise (*China Economic Times,* 2014). Zhuang Congsheng, in representing the private sector and entrepreneurial class, further commented that "what we want is not more allowances, but more fairness; we are not interested in privileges, but instead security." Here, he makes a clear distinction between privileges (and power), presumably achieved through political association, whether formally or informally; and security, achieved through the institutionalization of the rule of law. The article also noted concerns about the investment and operating environment for private entrepreneurs and their businesses, and how this is impacting their future. Zhuang said that "without vigorous legal protections, private enterprise is just a fragile commodity." He said that the cause of these problems is that officials have too much unchecked power and are not bound by the rule of law, and to attempt to counter this, entrepreneurs must spend excessive amounts of time attempting to win over officials. Moreover, prohibitive taxation, lack of access to necessary loans, and preferential treatment all add to their daily burden (*China Economic Times*, 2014).

This miasma of uncertainty and state predation, founded in China's lack of legal institutionalization, has led to an endless sea of economic calamity for China's private entrepreneurs. As the following article notes:

> The safety of entrepreneurs' property has not received adequate protection. Sometimes the government will issue a "confidential government document," typically resulting in the government's expropriation of most—if not all—of their property, the accumulation of which involves great pains and sacrifices. Just one year before the clause protecting private property was written into the constitution, the Shanxi local government adopted a "first accept the wells, and later criticize it" approach, whereby the government suddenly marched in and nationalized the thousands of oil wells that were the very foundation for the privately run and managed capital venture in Shanxi, even though the original reason for the Shanxi government's invitation and welcoming of these entrepreneurs was to "attract business and capital."
>
> Even though some entrepreneurs are able to rely on the support of local government, their security in the end is in no way guaranteed. Within the heavy chemical industry movement that surged in the twenty-first century, there was a Jiangsu entrepreneur, Dai Guofang, also known as "the private steel magnate," who under the vigorous support of the local government raised the quota of steel production from more than 200 tons to 840 tons, while boldly stating that "within three years they will outstrip *Baoshang Gangtie* [Company], and within five years will catch up with *Pu Xiang* [Company]."
>
> Nevertheless, in the spring of 2004, the centrally appointed inspection team concluded that they had "violated the law and regulations," and therefore Dai Guofang was arrested and charged with tax evasion. After undergoing his marathon trial, in April of 2004, Dai Guofang was charged with the crime of running a false receipt system used to reduce tax payments, and sentenced to five years in prison (Ma Guochuan, 2014).

Survey results show an overwhelming desire on the part of the entrepreneur for the implementation of policy and the construction of a legal framework that protects their right to private property. In one particular survey, for example, which surveyed 3258 respondents, 74.8 percent said one of the most immediate concerns is the need for the central government to implement policy that facilitates the construction of a more favorable environment for enterprise development. Moreover, entrepreneurs expressed significant concerns on the issue of enterprise expansion, specifically in the areas of acquiring loans and arbitrary governmental actions that negatively impact private enterprise. From the survey, 45.6 percent stated that there are significant problems with the issue of "clearly protecting rightful private property," specifically referring to added burdens, as noted above. A vast majority—82 percent of respondents—requested the strengthening of legislation in order to combat this problem (Zhang Houyi, 2008, 295–296).

At an informal meeting in July 1993, a representative of China's entrepreneurial class expressed the importance of legal institutionalization, specifically the *rule of law*, for the survival and growth of this class:

> To tell you the truth, many employers still have a lingering fear. They want to develop and increase their investment and use their expansion to further production. If you take great pains to struggle to make a comprehensive monetary investment, but you do not have legal protection, who can tread attentively and with concentration? So, only if there is the appearance of relevant laws and regulations can there be the healthy protection of the development of the private economy (Zhang Houyi, 1999, 273).

The author's interviews with entrepreneurs show that the absence of the rule of law, and adherence to the rule by law and pervasive state predation, has catalyzed the formation of property-law interests among the entrepreneurial class. In fact, the author's first interviewee, a middle-aged entrepreneur based in Beijing, expressed what he viewed as a government and government policies that are hostile towards the business class and their growth, and a legal system that is predicated on the rule by law, not the rule of law. In response to the question, "Do you feel that there are any factors which prevent you from maximizing on economic ventures and acquiring wealth?," he stated: "The government has policies that do not support the business class very well, and that is a problem. Also, taxation and tax policies create a lot of pressure for the business class" (Entrepreneur 1). He then proceeded by stating:

> We have private property and also have law regarding the private property. The problem is that the law which is supposed to protect this property is not well developed. . . . The legal system does not protect private property enough. In fact it is far from enough. Many Chinese people do not know how to protect themselves by the law like they do in the West. They don't know how to protect their

> interests. . . . From the government's perspective, they support the protection of private property—but the business class does not feel this (Entrepreneur 1).

His comment on the heavy burden of taxation imposed on the entrepreneurial class has been echoed by entrepreneurs elsewhere, such as in the following survey referenced in a Chinese news article, which found the following:

> They [the entrepreneurs] most closely follow and have the strongest opinion in the area of enterprise development. When asked what problems they follow most closely following the Sixteenth Party Congress, among the ten items mentioned the top four were as follows: 86.8 percent of the respondents chose "reform of the tax system"; 82.8 percent of respondents chose "to put in concrete terms in the constitution the protection of private property"; 82.2 percent of respondents mentioned "transforming the economic management function of government"; and 80.5 percent respondents mentioned "establishing a system of credit, a standard market arrangement" (Gu Jianjian, 2006).

In similar fashion, a young Beijing entrepreneur demonstrated his growing rationality, and resultant issues with the property-law environment in China, when he linked the deficiencies in the legal environment with the continuation of the one-party system:

> I think the multiparty system has its own advantages because the supervision and the control of all things is better. If it's a single party system, we can only move to one direction, the one that the party tells us. Our government makes a strategic decision, and the whole country follows it. Often the party has a perfect plan so to speak, but the execution of that plan is far from perfect; the bad supervision can bring a lot of new problems. That's why it's very important for our legal system to improve the control, supervision and execution (Entrepreneur 12).

Another Beijing-based entrepreneur echoed this sentiment when he said "Actually, this country does not belong to the emperor or an emperor-like person, but instead, it belongs to everybody. If they want society to become stable they must change" (Entrepreneur 5).

Among the interviews that the author conducted, several entrepreneurs highlighted their own specific experiences, and resultant frustration, related to the state's arbitrary intervention in their working environment, and the subsequent negative—and in many instances crushing—effects this posited on the entrepreneurs' businesses. One particular entrepreneur that the author interviewed in Shanghai, in response to the question "Do you feel there are any factors which prevent you from maximizing on economic ventures and acquiring wealth?," explained that there are economic opportunities and space for business growth, yet, this environment is met with a great deal of unpredictability, which can be traced back to China's legal and political institutions. Ultimately, this is a cause for concern among China's entrepreneurs:

> I think many business owners will pay attention to politics because I think that is a sign of where we are going. If your business is not going in the same direction as the government there can be walls that are hit. For example, 10 years ago when I was talking to my parents I believed that the industry for gaming and animation would make for a huge sale in China; but at the moment no one thinks that way. . . . Nowadays there are huge industries in China producing billions per day or per month, really. But this is primarily because the government has already realized it is an opportunity and that there is wealth in this industry. So, companies who are in business in this industry are receiving policy support from the government, and they may even be able to get taxes reduced or cut etc. But I was talking to an owner of a game developing company, and he was worried that maybe this won't last long because the government in the beginning wants this industry to grow, but this can change. If the government and its politics changes overnight and gaming is no longer favored, then guess what, so things like that can change the business around in a day. . . . So a lot of firms may close down because of this (Entrepreneur 7).

In similar fashion, a restaurant owner expressed significant frustration with the problems he has encountered in his attempts at enterprise expansion within one of China's largest cities. This particular entrepreneur had successfully created two businesses (a Western-oriented restaurant and a food additive import company) within a short period of time, and sought expansion of the restaurant business in other parts of this city. After expending large amounts of time researching the vast and dense compartments of the city, he identified one particular area that not only had availability for restaurant expansion, but that also promised significant potential based on what he was offering; he was given approval by city authorities as well. Nevertheless, in the end, the government arbitrarily intervened and prohibited him from opening a second restaurant in this particular area. In response to the question "Do you feel there are any factors which prevent you from maximizing on economic ventures and acquiring wealth?," he conveyed the following:

> There are some. The main one is related to government. For example, I am looking for other areas to open up additional branches of their restaurant. But in these areas, where there are little shops, the government doesn't let me open up a restaurant branch there, and in areas that I feel are very advantageous. The problem is that the law is not stable, and it changes every day. Some areas maybe 4 years ago I could set up a restaurant, but after 4 years I cannot set up the restaurant. . . . This is because the law changes all the time, and in my case it kept me from establishing my second restaurant. This is a very important factor (Entrepreneur 9).

> If you have some *guanxi*, if you are a leader in the government and you know this person, then you can set up the restaurant. Even if it is prohibited by law, if you know a government official in charge of that area then you can open the restaurant. I am of course not happy with this system. It is unfair. I work very hard (Entrepreneur 9).

His wife, who was sitting in on the interview and who is also involved in the business's operations, added the following comment to the discussion: "If you want to do business in China, you need to do a lot of socializing (dinners, drinking, etc.) with officials. So we spend a lot of time socializing—this is another business" (Entrepreneur 9). This entrepreneur's personal account reveals a core source of frustration common to many entrepreneurs: without this legal protection, officials with direct connections, or those in the private sector with indirect connections, can circumnavigate China's rule by law to their advantage, while those without recourse to these privileges are subjected to a constant tirade of extra-legal impositions and the arbitrary (legal) actions of officials.

Intellectual property rights were another issue highlighted in the course of the author's interviews. Baidu and Tencent, and their engagement in predatory behavior, and the costs they inflict on the entrepreneurial class, are but two examples worth mentioning. Baidu, the Chinese mega search engine, which has strong government connections and which engages in profiteering, has not surprisingly been able to survive where Google has failed. Baidu, for example, has allowed people to upload books by Chinese authors, which are then publicly accessible for download in Baidu's library collection, equating to copyright infringement (Entrepreneur 18; Lee, 2011). In similar fashion, Baidu violated record companies' rights when it allowed individuals to use its services to download music free of charge. They filed lawsuits in Beijing courts, but lost (Lee, 2011).

Tencent is notorious for profiteering, specifically targeting China's entrepreneurial class. On the surface they are a "social media company" (Entrepreneur 18; Entrepreneur 17). Behind the scenes, Tencent is run by China's privileged elite and princelings, engaging in extensive predatory behavior (Witness 17). As one entrepreneur indicated in an interview:

> Do you know Tencent? This is a tech giant—just to copycat every product with great market potential. They hunt for startups with a good idea and pretend to be interested in investing. They send someone to conduct interviews, learn about the company, and then follow up by alerting their in house engineers to try and copy it. It's a very dangerous playground to build your startup, but everyone is looking at its rewards, even though very few can make it. The potential is too good to give up. So money is continuing to pour in—especially in the mobile Internet field (Entrepreneur 17).

Another entrepreneur explained the unfair and inadequate nature of China's legal environment:

> After it [Baidu] grows bigger, it contributed considerable taxation to government. And then our government gave it more protection in every possible way to keep it safe in market competition with other players like Google. In return, Baidu was doing very good in information filtering to guarantee that the search results the users obtained were aligned with the voice of the mainstream media under government control. And this is also a very important reason why Google failed in China (Entrepreneur 18).

> There are a lot of similar examples here such as Tencent Group, the largest social media company in China. When it survived in the early stages, the government intervened to give it protection which made the market competition unfair. So when these kind of companies grow and finally become kinds of giants in their industries, their relationship with the local governments has been very solid with a lot of deals under table. These giants then easily bully the small start-up companies without considering the intellectual property issues, etc. (Entrepreneur 18).

Many interviewees indicated at some point in the interview that China's wealth was reaching only a minority of the population, while a majority of the population was still without the benefits of China's market reforms. At first the author interpreted this as their description of the dichotomy between the urban and rural areas in China, and thus a continued lack of developmental reach from coastal to inland areas; but this was not the meaning of their comments. Instead, their comments were intended to refer to the level of official corruption in China and the extent to which they squeeze the entrepreneur and extract profits and resources from them in order to fill their personal coffers. As one entrepreneur indicated in his response to the question "How would you characterize the relationship between your business and the government? Do you have good and beneficial relations; or are there some issues?": "There is a relationship. They help the small business owners, because they help you invest your money. Small businesses help employ people and deal with problems, so the government invests in these businesses. But when they get rich the government takes the profit from them. They invest in businesses now, but then take profit away" (Entrepreneur 9).

One particular entrepreneur highlighted this connection between opportunity, lack of the rule of law, official corruption, and ultimately the increasing burdens and corruption directed toward the entrepreneurial class. In other words, though many opportunities exist, without the rule of law and within the continuation of a one-party system, there also exists an increasing host of problems for China's entrepreneurs. When asked, "How do you feel about China's new market economy and new societal wealth?," she responded:

> A lot of opportunities—the number on the paper looks very well now. But I'm not sure about the reality, what is really going on inside of China. There are a lot of problems with economic development. One of the KPI's (key performance indicators) for local officials is GDP. So you always see that the GDP numbers look like perfect numbers on paper—some are real and some are not real. If they can get GDP higher, then they can also get a higher position, and with a higher position they can get more power and more chance to steal money. So everyone tries to make up the GDP stats. So definitely our country has grown up a lot in the past 10 or 15 years, a huge difference compared to before, but there is a lot of potential danger too. Overall I am concerned; small companies will start to lose business because of taxes and difficulty raising money to develop their business. But in China the economy depends on these small businesses. For example, recently a couple of factories in Jiangsu province shut down and redirected their capital into the stock market etc. because it was too much pressure for them within this type of environment to run the factories. Small companies have a very difficult time raising money, so they use illegal financing. For example, I am one, I collect money—I know a lot of rich guys. But it is illegal (Entrepreneur 14).

A third entrepreneur to express his economically calamitous encounter with the party-state apparatus was a man who had established an advertising firm with two other individuals in one of China's largest cities. While in his previous position he observed the growth of the sphere of economic freedom, and the opportunities that were proliferating, which inspired him to start his own firm and enter the world of entrepreneurship. Although he was optimistic about this new venture, he initially struggled to profit from this newly established enterprise. Not surprisingly, he attributed his lack of growth and success to China's rule by law and its arbitrary nature. As he explained:

> When we started our business, you know, we are technology-based company so we apply a patent to protect our software. But we find it cannot protect anything, because the market—the very rich market—in it there exist too many competitors and no rule of law. So to be honest in China the property protection, such as intellectual properties, is only a slogan; no one abides by the law. Most of the people break the law (Entrepreneur 10).

As a result, his business was severely affected. As he described:

> The policy, the government policy creates problems for me. For example, before the financial crisis, the Shanghai government made a decision that all outdoor

> advertisement would be cancelled, particularly before the Shanghai Expo. So many of the small and middle advertising businesses had to shut down. The government did not want all the commotion of advertising in Shanghai around the expo, so this kind of outdoor advertising was prohibited. They wanted to keep clear the Shanghai streets—no sort of mass advertising. Moreover, Internet in China is so limited. About 3 years ago the CCP started to review the content of every website strictly, so many websites disappeared. Around more than 50 percent of websites of middle and small websites disappeared during that period. So it is very risky when you run a small business in China. You are always confronted with these kinds of risks (Entrepreneur 10).

In fact, this particular entrepreneur was not afraid to voice his opinion and frustration over clashes between his business and the party-state's arbitrary legal environment. In response to the following two questions "Do you feel that China's legal system adequately protects your property?" and "Is it possible to effectively administer the rule of law inside a single party system? If not, what is the solution," he stated, respectively: "It is a slogan of government, just a slogan. Single-party is the root. You know the CCP I think are hooligans. They are the problem; they are the reason why the rule of law and private property are only slogans and do not adequately exist in society. The government only protects their own benefits" (Entrepreneur 10).

Finally, three different entrepreneurs indicated how property in China is not private and protected, but instead, is always available to the state for the taking, and how this in turn, has significantly profound consequences for business growth and investment. One entrepreneur, in response to the question "What is your understanding of private property? Does private property exist in China?," stated:

> No. In China things are very different. If you get rich, and you want to invest, then the methods are very different: the government makes them rich and expands their business, but at the same time the government takes all the businesses' harvest and it is easy for the government to do this. One minute you can be rich and the next poor because of this . . . so for my property this has a big influence; the business may be big, but the profit small because the government takes this. I will invest my money into other businesses etc. but I will lose this money because the government will take it away (Entrepreneur 9).

Yet another Shanghai entrepreneur responded to this question with not only a definitive "No," but she furthermore articulated what is required if China's rampant corruption is to be eliminated and the system of the rule by law is to be replaced with the rule of law:

> The Chinese government robs and takes property, and will use all kinds of different excuses to take it away. Did you know that even if you die in China

> and want to buy a burial spot, you can only get the right for 20 years? Either you are refunded, or if they cannot find kin, they just throw it away and use the land. And also the land is always owned by the government and housing for example is only yours for 70 years. Everyone knows it (noncompliance with the law) isn't right, but everyone still does it because they know they can't survive without it. I used to talk to my husband and I told him that if you don't do this you will not have any business. He said I don't want to do that. He said I hate that. I want to come here and help the Chinese make changes. I said alright, do you know the meaning of revolution? It means somebody needs to lose blood, some people need to lose heads. You come here to make money, if you want to do that—great do that. Maybe after two generations revolution will happen, but it will not change for a long time (Entrepreneur 14).

When asked the same question ("What is your understanding of private property? Does private property exist in China?") in an interview in the spring of 2012, one particular entrepreneur responded with veritable frustration, more so than in any other interview the author conducted. These were his words:

> Yes of course we have big problems. Registering for example: so you have to 1) find an agency who will charge you for the services because they have very special relations with the government; 2) do it by yourself! [there was sarcasm on his part as he inferred this is not an option] You have to do it 1, 2, 3, 4, 5, 6 times and on and on. Also right now I am continuing to deal with what happens after you register: all of your personal information will be released, which is then followed by endless solicitations. Also once you register you are forced to pay money to attend training to learn how to pay taxes; yet everyone already knows how to do this—it is just a money-maker. Also to pay taxes they forced me to buy a device to pay my taxes, costing 2,500 RMB; and before ever using the device I was informed that the device was no longer needed and now I was told I have to buy a whole different device for another 2,500 RMB. All required by the tax bureau. The manufacturer of the device is a family member of one of the government officials (Entrepreneur 18).

One particular entrepreneur indicated that although China has improved and transformed markedly in terms of its economic growth, quality of life and societal differentiation, in many other areas there are serious concerns, most notably in the area of legal institutionalization (Entrepreneur 14). In her words:

> The entrepreneurs are very desperate. The truth is if you want to do well you need to have a lot of good government relationships. And you need to make a lot of dirty deals with them. For us we feel it isn't right, but we have no choice if you want to run and expand companies. Also I heard from some of my friends that it isn't that you only don't get enough support from the local government, but also if their business begins to run very well the local officials will feel jealous, and if

> that official's brother or sister want to run that business, they will even try their best to take it away (Entrepreneur 14).

An entrepreneur once said to the author that "my generation has the mentality of 'you are not taking away my property—we won't let it happen'" (Entrepreneur 16). Chinese entrepreneurs' views regarding China's current legal system, particularly the *Baling Hou* generation, that it's unpredictable and arbitrary, seem to be animated by routine encounters with arbitrary enforcement and actions of (local) authorities—and the damage it causes to their business operations. The comment by this particular entrepreneur signals a deep frustration over the current system of law—so much so that this particular entrepreneur is determined not to allow these arbitrary actions to take place. Thus, this begs the question: to what extent has a liberal-political entrepreneurial class—a bourgeoisie in the political sense of the term—emerged in China?

CONCLUSION

This chapter examined the second phase in the liberal evolution of a Chinese entrepreneurial class: the nature of China's extant legal system, particularly the extent to which it is characterized by official malfeasance and organizational corruption, and from this whether an entrepreneurial class with specific property-law interests has emerged. The Chinese Communist Party has pursued some institutional reforms, both legal and political, most notably those of the Deng Xiaoping and Jiang Zemin eras which circumscribed tenure of political office and to some degree de-politicized and de-militarized political organs. Nevertheless, legal reforms have proven superficial, and China continues to lack a system of law that protects the individual and restrains the state. Indeed, corruption is endemic in China and cases of corruption in general, and those affecting the entrepreneurial class in particular, abound. They have little guarantee that their property, wealth, and capital, will be protected, and face an unpredictable business environment and constant impediments.

Indeed, the consequence of this for the party, at least the social consequence, is what appears to be the rise of an entrepreneurial class increasingly antagonistic toward what they deem to be a predatory state and an unpredictable legal system, and the potential for political consequences if these issues remain unaddressed. The author's interviews with entrepreneurs show that they possess a long list of grievances directly related to the lack of the rule of law, and many have articulated their awareness of the link between these grievances and the current nature of China's legal and political institutions. Whether they are forming liberal-political values that they deem as necessary for securing their property-law interests, and acting on these values, is the subject of the following chapter.

Chapter Six

China's Private Entrepreneurs

The Formation of Liberal Political Values?

INTRODUCTION

This chapter examines the entrepreneur's response to the lack of legal institutionalization and resultant corruption and state predation discussed in the previous chapter. That is, it analyzes the entrepreneurial class's level of political awareness, scale of participation in political institutions and party membership, degree of individual and organizational agency, and emigration trends and characteristics. The author first examines the *Baling Hou* generation, including what makes them unique and how *Baling Hou* entrepreneurs might be more likely to pursue political agency. The author then assesses party membership among this class and involvement in formal political posts. Whether or not they intend to wed with the party-state is an important indicator of future political agency and prospects for political change. Finally, the author will examine whether they are resolved to remain in China, and organize around their interests and act in support of them, or more inclined to simply flee the country to resolve their current—and growing—crisis. Ultimately, the author seeks to determine the extent to which China's entrepreneurial class has evolved through the third and final phase of liberalism, that is, exhibiting specific political values and an understanding of the political origins of their problems, and an intent to organize and act in support of these interests.

ENTREPRENEURS' POLITICAL ORIENTATION AND PARTICIPATION IN POLITICAL INSTITUTIONS

The *Baling Hou* Generation and Private Entrepreneurs' Political Awareness

China's *Baling Hou* entrepreneurs possess a distinct identity and are a relatively understudied demographic among China's middle class. The *Baling Hou* generation has been clearly demarcated from past generations, most of all for their level of independence and activity—such as social activism, use of Internet mediums, and criticism of political abuses of power (Zhu, Shan, and Hu (ZSH), 2011; Jing Lin and Xiaoyan Sun, 2010). They are otherwise known as the "Torch Generation" or the "Bird's Nest Generation" possessing a particular aptitude for "independent thought" (ZSH, 2011, 327). An article on the *Baling Hou* generation noted the specific liberal characteristics of this generation and characterized this group as embodying and promoting autonomy and market growth; as active in their communities; as "Netizens," or "active participants in the cyber world" and as active in utilizing the Internet for information and as a vehicle to drive their concerns; and as "twice as likely to microblog and to blog and video conference" (Jing Lin and Xiaoyan Sun, 2010, 234–235).

A general survey on the *Baling Hou* generation produced by the Chinese Academy of Social Sciences, which surveyed the orientation of their political values, revealed that liberal political characteristics are beginning to define this class. As a result of the potential sensitivity of the findings, the report was published internally and thus is not widely accessible. Some of the findings, presented in an article by Stanley Rosen, reveal the following liberal values among the *Baling Hou* generation: "In terms of belief systems, 72.7 percent chose 'individual struggle' . . . more than 61 percent identified with liberalism (*ziyou zhuyi*, 自由主义) and found it to be a concept of universal moral significance . . . [and] close to 36 percent of respondents endorsed the concept of 'separation of powers' " (2009, 366).

The author's interviews with entrepreneurs in Beijing and Shanghai, most of which were either *Baling Hou* entrepreneurs or individuals born just before 1980, revealed a similar degree of liberal political values and political awareness to that of the *Baling Hou* generation discussed above. A number of entrepreneurs the author interviewed expressed their desire to follow political news and to maintain their political awareness, yet indicated a lack of interest in becoming a party member or assuming a formal political post. For example, an interviewee in Beijing conveyed the following: "I pay a lot of attention to politics but I am not interested in it. I pay a lot of attention to the issues, but I don't want to get involved in it. I pay close attention to it on the news, but I don't want to join politics" (Entrepreneur 1). Another Beijing-based entrepreneur stated: "I watch politics on TV and read about it in the newspaper and on the Internet. I do this to be aware" (Entrepreneur 3). When the author asked a third Beijing-based entrepreneur "Are you interested in China's politics? Do you think business-people should take an interest in politics; or is it best to keep politics and business separate?," he responded in the following way: "Every Chinese is interested in politics. . . . Right now everyone is watching *Xinwen Lianbo* (新闻联播), a most popular program on CCTV. They like to watch this. I am interested in being aware and watching, but not interested in becoming a politician. Right now it is not our time, maybe after 100 years it will be" (Entrepreneur 5). Other entrepreneurial responses to the question included "Yes and most business people are and should be" (Entrepreneur 7); and "Of course the business people should be interested and aware of what is happening with politics. It is a very important market intelligence" (Entrepreneur 10).

Interviews with entrepreneurs also indicated consciousness of liberal political values and the need for their institutionalization, including, reference to democratization and a multiparty system, which reflected a desire for the right to vote; the importance of the separation of powers within the political system in order to prevent abuse of political power; and the freedom of speech and press, indicated in their growing use of Internet mediums in the absence of alternative modes of free information gathering and space for freely expressing opinions. The foundation for entrepreneurs' embracement of liberal political values is the growing intervention of party officials in the economic sphere, particularly, abuses of political power which have compromised their full rights to private property. In turn, the common theme that emerged from the interviews in terms of liberal political values is the entrepreneurs' recognition of the need to introduce mechanisms to check the power of officials. Thus, entrepreneurs have indicated a growing demand for new and liberal political institutions.

One interesting finding from the author's interviews was an understanding among many of these entrepreneurs that the party is only responsible to internal persons and entities, not to society as a whole, and thus abuses abound, which stands in stark contrast to the party's claims of its high morality. In an interview with one particular Beijing-based entrepreneur, he stated: "We have representatives for the elections, but normal people don't know much about these people, they don't have enough information. There are a lot of reforms in China, but the intention behind the reforms are for the government to protect its own interests so it doesn't matter if these reforms are good for the people or not" (Entrepreneur 1). Interviews with Shanghai-based entrepreneurs yielded a high number of similar responses. In one interview, when asked "Is it possible to effectively administer the rule of law inside a single party system? If not, what is the solution?," he stared at the question for at least a minute without answering. I proceeded to tell him he could skip over this question if he wished. He said "no I will answer it," and after another minute or so, and a blushed look over his face, he stated "this is a very sensitive question"—(Entrepreneur 9) and we moved on.

Two interviews conducted with separate Shanghai entrepreneurs revealed similar responses. In response to the question "What is your view on corruption in China? Do you feel a need for the rule of law in order to limit corruption and protect your property?," one entrepreneur stated "*guanxi* and relationships are at the heart of corruption and ultimately the one-party system. It's all connection based and one person only answers to their boss, etc. There are no checks and balances—they wield so much power. It's only under a very few cases that the law is explicit and doesn't allow for corruption, but the vast majority are grey and therefore encourage corruption" (Entrepreneur 16). In a second interview with a Shanghai-based entrepreneur, when asked "Is it possible to effectively administer the rule of law inside a single party system? If not, what is the solution?," he stated: "I can fix some bugs, but not all so I have a fundamental problem, the government, which can come up with new rules at any time to control the industry. Thus, there is a saying in China: "To make money is easy, to keep money safe is difficult." At the end of the interview he stated: "It also goes back to the party—it is unfair" (Entrepreneur 18).

As a result of this emerging awareness of the problems in China in general, and the root of these problems in particular, that is, the one-party system, China's entrepreneurs are beginning to think, discuss—and even value—the democratic process. In response to the question "Do you think that China will retain a single party system for a long time?," a Beijing-based entrepreneur responded with the following: "I think in the future it is going to be a multiparty system, but not for another 20 years. Maybe nothing will change for another 20–30 years. The Chinese society has to change first" (Entrepreneur 12). An interview with a Shanghai-based entrepreneur yielded a much more explicit reference to the democratic process. In response to the question, "Do you think the government will introduce direct elections for people's congresses?; Would you support this move now; and what is your impression on the views of businesspeople on this question?," he stated: "Impossible! I am very certain. I think it [direct elections] is a good idea, but it is impossible at the moment—maybe 5 years later, or 10 years later. It is of course a very good idea for my business" (Entrepreneur 10). He then went on to say:

> I think democratization [民主化]. Maybe in the very near future, within 10 years, I really think. I don't think there will be a revolution, but I think there will be democratic political reform; and I hope that the entrepreneurs will have

> a big part of this. The darkness before some reform . . . maybe 10 years later we will become another US or UK. I think people will live better than now, but entrepreneurs must have a more friendly environment instead of struggling to break even. You know most of the profits are taken by the government, through taxation and many other ways; and small and middle businesses are scratched (Entrepreneur 10).

One particular interviewee in Shanghai demonstrated depth in her understanding of the endemic problems within China's one-party system, specifically observed in her mentioning repeatedly the phrase "dirty politics" in reference to the party-state and its depth of corruption, and ultimately the problems this presents for the entrepreneurial class. When asked "Are you interested in politics? Do you think businesspeople should take an interest in politics; or is it best to keep politics and business separate?," she replied,

> Chinese politics are dirty. When I was twelve years old I already knew that Chinese politics were very dirty—it is a very dirty game. Do you know why? In China's schools they always have different kinds of levels. They call it kids officers. It is very complicated—they learn from Russia. Each school has a pioneers system—the number one student represents the whole pioneers and he or she should be the model. Actually, they announce that this person was selected by the students, and each party gives a speech and the students can come to vote. But teachers like kids like me. I will not be too dangerous, I will not be a big mouth girl, and I will study well. One of the teachers had an individual meeting with me and said 'if you are selected as the number one student, what will you do?' . . . if . . . right! [laughing]. I knew I was not very popular and I knew I would not be selected by the students. But when my teacher asked me that, when I was 12, I told my father I will be elected for this position, because everything is fake in China if you talk about elections, politics—everything is fake . . . so I was elected but it was not a real election. If the government says 'A' we will understand it as 'B' or 'C'—as we don't believe it (Entrepreneur 14).

Furthermore, when asked "Do you think the government will introduce direct elections for people's congresses? Would you support this move now; and what is your impression of the views of businesspeople on this matter?," she stated,

> They already announce that they are doing that [laughing]. Unless they lose power and are kicked out, they will never do that. . . . Some people say we need to wait until the country is managed by the *Baling Hou* generation. I think when the *Baling Hou* are in their 40s—in 15 more years—that we might have a chance. But the dangerous thing is that we have too long of a history, and as soon as you get power, maybe they too start to enjoy the power in their hands. . . . I recently got a chance to watch an interesting documentary on Tiananmen

> Square in 1989. The woman making the documentary is American but grew up in China . . . one point she made concerned the students who tried to organize and fight against the government: one of the protestors (called Chai Ling), who was suggested for the Nobel Peace Prize and who was a student leader at Beijing University, began to develop into those people who get the power in our country and all do exactly the same thing, because we are raised this way—in a way that encourages one who acquires power to take advantage of it. But this is twenty years later and things are different and the hope is in the *Baling Hou* generation . . . I hate this system and I wish it can change (Entrepreneur 14).

Thus, findings from the author's interviews indicates that at least a portion of China's *Baling Hou* generation of entrepreneurs are aware of the endemic problems caused by China's one-party system, and its intent on remaining unreformed. Most importantly, they seem to be developing political awareness and political values that are consistent with an open political system that is accountable and which grants significant power to society, as a result of their ongoing cleavage with the state. They also seem to demonstrate an understanding of where these problems originate, and why they continue to persist. However, are they simply contemplating these political concepts, or are they determined to engage in organizational and political agency to realize their property-law interests and to ensure a predictable business environment? If so, through what channels and mediums will they proceed? These questions will be the focus of the following sections.

Private Entrepreneurs' Party Membership and Participation in Formal Political Posts

As mentioned earlier, Jiang Zemin's speech and announcement in 2001 was historic in that it welcomed entrepreneurs—historically seen as enemies of the state—into the party, yet, even after the party lifted the ban in 2001, evidence shows that the party was unsuccessful in genuinely culling private entrepreneurs into its ranks. Consider the following categories in which the identity of both private entrepreneur and party member meet: 1) those who were first party members and then private entrepreneurs, that is, party members who were intent on diving into the private sector and entrepreneurship but were prohibited to do so until 2001; 2) those who were first managers of SOEs before embarking on a path of private entrepreneurship through SOE conversion; and 3) those who were private entrepreneurs before garnering any party affiliation, and who typically did so for access to resources and privileges, considering the continued absence of the rule of law (Zhang Houyi, 2011; Zhang Houyi and Liu Pingqing, 2004b; Zhang Houyi, 2008).

According to the Eighth National Private Enterprise Sample Survey, 87.7 percent of those who joined the party did so prior to 2001 (in other words prior to Jiang Zemin's speech calling on entrepreneurs to join the party) (Zhang Houyi, 2011, 281). Further, the main factor behind the increase in party membership was the conversion of state-owned enterprises, particularly, at the end of the 1990s where many SOEs, including township and village enterprises and small and medium enterprises, were transformed into private enterprises, and thus the resulting shift from managers of state-owned enterprises to private entrepreneurs (Zhang Houyi and Liu Pingqing, 2004b). Indeed, as Zhang Houyi notes:

> Why in the previous four surveys did the proportion of private entrepreneurs who had obtained party membership not exceed 20 percent, yet beginning with the fifth survey forward (beginning in 2001) jump to above 30 percent? Based on analysis of the Fifth National Sample Survey, the main reasons rest in the period following the 1990s, where many SOEs (rural village and township level enterprises, urban collective enterprises, and small and medium enterprises) carried out reforms whereby SOEs were converted into private enterprises. But many of the enterprise managers of the SOEs were originally party members (Zhang Houyi, 2008, 298).

According to one survey, which drew on 833 enterprises, 422 of the enterprises' leading cadres were already party members (Zhang Houyi, 2008, 298). In fact, according to the Fifth National Private Enterprise Survey (in 2002), over 90 percent of private entrepreneurs had entered the party prior to establishing their businesses (again due to the reform of SOEs) (Zhang Houyi, 2008, 299). Further, in a survey conducted of 565 party entrepreneurs, 47.3 percent of the respondents noted that their previous post was in an SOE: 18.5 percent from national SOEs, 14.9 percent from the city and township collectives enterprises, and 13.9 percent from the village level enterprises (Zhang Houyi and Chen Guangjin, 2002, 93). As Zhang Houyi notes: "It seems that these state-owned institutions furnished many of the resources that are indispensable for the creation of their enterprises" (Zhang Houyi and Chen Guangjin, 2002, 93).

In addition to the phenomenon whereby previous managers of state owned enterprises assume the new identity of private entrepreneur when a SOE is converted, and thus simply continue their allegiance to the state and their party membership, another scenario exists where entrepreneurs were first party members before deciding on an entrepreneurial career. In a *Huanqiu Shibao* article, Zhao Min speaks of his personal experience. Zhao Min, who formerly worked at the Foreign Ministry of Economics and Trade, links himself to what he calls the "92' group," referring to the impact of Deng Xiaoping's 1992 tour which re-activated the economy following setbacks related to events in Tiananmen Square. In particular, he notes that this reactivation of the economy formed the seeds which would later sprout into the party's formal acceptance in 2001 of China's private entrepreneurs, and which in turn allowed him to change from the "red road" of a government official to the "business road." As he noted, "previously there was a document which stipulated that managers of privately run enterprises had to leave the party. But the 'Three Represents' resolved this problem, allowing entrepreneurs such as myself to continue to stay in the party" (Haunqiu Shibao, 2011). Thus, following the party's adjustment of its policy toward private entrepreneurs, in terms of the influx of members from the ranks of the entrepreneurial class, many seem to have come from either previous managers of SOEs or from existing party members who were unauthorized to both retain party membership and engage in entrepreneurial activities.

Moreover, the proportion of entrepreneurs that claim party membership is relatively low, and again, this is prior to factoring in the aforementioned characteristics of many of the private entrepreneurs who are also party members. Zhang Houyi notes that party membership as an avenue for political participation has received limited interest among entrepreneurs (Zhang Houyi, 2008). For example, although the number of entrepreneurs who joined the party rose between 1993 and 2002, the proportion of private entrepreneurs who joined the party remained relatively low, and the number decreased from 2004 to 2006: 1993: 13.1 percent; 1995: 17.1 percent; 1997: 16.6 percent; 2000: 19.8 percent; 2002: 29.9 percent; 2004: 33.9 percent; 2006: 32.2 percent (Zhang Houyi, 2008, 298). According to the Fifth National Sample Survey, in the seven year period following Jiang Zemin's 2001 speech, only a small number of entrepreneurs had joined the party: 70 percent of the respondents indicated no party membership, and only 10 percent of these respondents indicated a future desire to join the party (Zhang Houyi, 2008, 298; Zhang Houyi and Liu Pingqing, 2004b, 48). According to the Eighth National Sample Survey, out of 4098 respondents, only 1372, or 33.5 percent, had joined the party (Zhang Houyi, 2011, 281). According to data from Shenzhen, since August 2001, the party has added over 5000 members each year on average, yet, private entrepreneurs represent a negligible 9 out of these 5000 new members. According to a survey conducted in Guangdong Province, of 100 private entrepreneurs surveyed, only 31 were party members; of the 69 that lacked party membership, half indicated no desire to join the party and one-quarter indicated a sense of ambivalence toward future membership (Zhang Houyi and Liu Pingqing, 2004b, 48). Finally, when in a survey entrepreneurs were asked "How do you improve your political position?," only 11.1 percent answered "I strive to join the CCP" (Zhang Houyi, 2008, 296–297).

The same holds true with the entrepreneurs' involvement in state organs: involvement is relatively limited. Zhang Houyi and Liu Pingqing have shown that formal-dependent avenues of political participation (party membership or formal political posts) are undesired modes of participation for entrepreneurs, while informal-independent activity is on the rise (2004). In surveying 565 entrepreneurs regarding their participation in people's congresses, only 17.4 percent indicated involvement; in surveying 1,143 entrepreneurs regarding their participation in the CPPCC, only 35.1 percent indicated involvement. On the other hand, in surveying 2,712 entrepreneurs, 83.4 percent indicated their involvement in the association of industry and commerce; and when surveying 1,562 entrepreneurs, 48 percent indicated involvement in either a private association or the Association of Private Businessmen (Chen Guangjin, 2002, 46).

A survey carried out in 2005 by the Media and Research Center of the Chinese Academy of Social Sciences in some of the largest urban centers in China (Beijing, Shanghai, Shenyang and Guangzhou), which asked citizens about their level of participation in their respective communities, revealed similar findings concerning the types of political and civic participation that are most important to ordinary citizens. The activities that attracted the highest degree of interest and participation were "community work" and "participation in elections," while "participation in local government activities" and "participation in party activities" were not deemed as important forms of civic participation. In other words, respondents indicated an interest in political awareness and staying current on political events and developments, as well as the importance of their participation in political elections, but not in participating directly in party activities, including membership, or serving in formal positions of government (Wang Junxiu, 2006, 70–72).

Indeed, when respondents were asked about their interest in participating in the process of electing members of people's congresses, some 36 percent said that they are "quite interested." Moreover, this growing interest is not arbitrary; instead, respondents pointed to specific reasons that act as motivating forces, namely the impact elections have on economic development, on improving the quality of life of participants, and on the supervision of officials. In fact a different survey found that participation was highest in those activities that were related to the economic interests of the participants: 87.2 percent of the respondents stated that they "very much wish" or "rather wish" to participate in these activities. Thus, participating in "property owners' committees," especially for those who own homes or businesses, was far higher than participation in other activities, namely activities outside the spheres of individual rights and economic interests (Wang Junxiu, 2006, 72–73).

Furthermore, individuals who are private entrepreneurs first, who are members of the *Baling Hou* generation, and who run small-scale enterprises (fewer than 50 employees), do not seem interested in party membership.

Interviews conducted by the author revealed an entrepreneurial class simply disinterested in affiliation with the party. For example, consider the following responses from entrepreneurs interviewed in response to the question "Are you involved in the CCP?:" "No. I never thought to become a CCP member" (Entrepreneur 1); "I am not a CCP member, but many members of the older generation are members of the CCP" (Entrepreneur 2); "No . . . I was going to become a CCP member, but I made a bit of a mistake. Now I am not interested in becoming a CCP member" (Entrepreneur 3); "No" (Entrepreneurs 4, 5, 8, 9, 10, 11, 12); "No. For many this is a bad arrangement—too much money is expended as a result of this arrangement" (Entrepreneur 6);

> No, but my dad is. He is secretary in the party over a school. Interestingly, my dad hasn't encouraged me to become a CCP member. Before there was a huge effect to becoming a CCP member and it use to be hard to get into the party. But nowadays . . . many people are really concerned about whether I get good pay, etc. Before business owners were considered capitalists which were considered bad—that is related to the Cultural Revolution. Maybe 10 years after no one talks about it anymore. But really there wasn't anything on paper that said those people could join the party; so that [2001 when Jiang Zemin announced the welcoming of entrepreneurs into the party] was a moment where now those business owners can officially join if they want. It isn't forced; but for a younger generation, and people like me, we don't think in that way, we don't care so much. It is certainly related to your background (Entrepreneur 7).

"No. But even if offered I wouldn't accept it because my grandfather used to be a KMT officer, a provincial mayor, and he was executed by the CCP. Even graduates don't care about membership—it is only out of necessity. Most fortunes are controlled by the government, whether you are directly in the system or not" (Entrepreneur 14). I then followed up on his comment with the question—"where are they getting this money from?" He responded with the following:

> Depends on what kind of power you have. For example if you work for the fire bureau—how can you get your money? In China if you want to build something you have to put a fire system in there. You can buy whatever product you want to buy; but before you start to sell this building you must get approval from the fire bureau's leader. Some of the guys who use the local cheap, [poor] quality products can get approval so easily; yet those who use the high quality products don't get approved—you know why? Because if you pay me. For example if you work for the education bureau how can you get money? Well you need a license to open the school, right. No matter how well you did, with preparations, buildings, teachers, they can always find excuses not to give you the license. Some people have fake companies registered—with nothing there; it is so dirty here (Entrepreneur 14).

"No" (Entrepreneur 16).

On the other hand, evidence suggests that private entrepreneurs are actively establishing their own intermediary organizations to protect their interests and to find ways to collaborate. The development of this organizational activity can be observed as early as 1993, when the privatization of the economy accelerated. Zhang Houyi, for example, noted that "beginning in 1993, entrepreneurs formed trade associations for private enterprises in certain cities and provinces, such as Guangdong," and that according to a survey "80.7 percent of entrepreneurs surveyed believed that they needed to establish their own industry trade association" (Zhang Houyi, 1999, 274). Pursuing the formation of these trade associations and other associational activities was one of the several "political demands" of China's private entrepreneurs (Zhang Houyi, 1999, 269–275). Among the reasons for pursuing these political demands, two were most notable: "to seek political support for the protection of their lawful rights and interests" and "to seek an effective vehicle to realize their own values" (Zhang Houyi, 1999, 275). According to another report, a national survey conducted among entrepreneurs found that more than 80 percent of respondents indicated it was "necessary to establish their own trade association or club" (Zhang Houyi and Liu Pingqing, 2004).

Although not indicative of widespread associational activity, its mere existence in various areas provided evidence of the entrepreneur's rationality and the recognition of and response to China's lack of legal institutionalization, and even the potential to be a political force. Indeed as Zhang Houyi notes in his conclusion "the existence and development of the private entrepreneurial group is not only an important socioeconomic force, but also likely to develop into a political force that cannot be ignored" (Zhang Houyi, 1999, 275). A more recent yet increasingly powerful mechanism through which entrepreneurs are exercising their voice is through Internet mediums, particularly microblogs. The following section will examine the extent to which China's entrepreneurs are exercising their voice, and the extent to which they are simply fleeing China, in response to widespread state predation and an unpredictable operating environment.

FIGHT OR FLIGHT? RIGHTS-BASED AGENCY AND EMIGRATION AMONG CHINA'S ENTREPRENEURS

This section will address the following key question: how are China's entrepreneurs responding to the aforementioned state predation toward entrepreneurs, and their enterprises and private property, especially if they aren't flooding into the party apparatus? In particular, are they simply satisfied with the status quo, emigrating out of China, or exercising some type of individual and organizational agency, in an effort to further their class interests?

Emigration Trends among Private Entrepreneurs

R. Bin Wong and Jean-Laurent Rosenthal have analyzed the historical phenomenon whereby individuals respond, typically in one of two ways, to regimes that impose high rates of taxation: through what they term "exit" or "voice" (2011, 187):

> Exit, for our present purposes, refers to a variety of strategies that deprive the ruler of revenue without confrontation when individuals decide that they do not like their leaders' behavior. It includes people emigrating to another country that might offer a better mix of public spending and private opportunities . . . there are also other ways, more effective and more expensive, to get the attention of the ruler; these we will call *voice*. They include both institutions whose assent is required for new taxes . . . and organized protests and revolts (2011, 187).

This point is important and relevant to the case of contemporary China in that much discussion has ensued over how China's entrepreneurs respond to the party's predation, which here exists in the form of not only high taxation, but also in the extra legal fines and levies, and other forms of extra-legal taxation, that are imposed on entrepreneurs, as well as outright arrogation of property. Do they exercise their "voice?" That is, do they desire to remain in China, and to protest against these abuses? Or do they simply "exit" by emigrating out of China?

Some of China's private entrepreneurs are responding to the country's lack of legal institutionalization by simply leaving China, taking with them both their property and ideas, among other things. Yet, what are the characteristics of these entrepreneurs that decide to leave China, and on what scale are they exiting? According to surveys, the individuals most likely to emigrate are the ultra wealthy (Wang, 2013; *China Economic Times*, 2014; Tang Xiangyang and Cao Xingbi, 2013). According to one survey, "56 percent of respondents in this group said they are considering emigrating, or already emigrated from China" (Wang, 2013). China's International Immigration Report found similar behavior among China's wealthy entrepreneurs. According to this report, among entrepreneurs worth over 100 million *yuan*, "27 percent have already immigrated and 47 percent are in the process of considering immigrating" and among entrepreneurs worth over 10 million *yuan*, "nearly 60 percent have already completely immigrated by investing or have considered something related" (*China Economic Times*, 2014). A survey carried out by China's *Jingji Guancha* (*Economic Observer*) also questioned entrepreneurs about their interest in emigrating. Of the entrepreneurs surveyed, "45.71 percent revealed that they have already or are in the process of planning their emigration" (Tang Xiangyang and Cao Xingbi, 2013).

Several predominating factors have motivated these wealthy entrepreneurs to leave China. One reason is simply the amenities and overall high quality of life that is available in Western developed countries, including predictable and stable institutions through which investments can be made. In particular, many entrepreneurs seek to provide their children with quality education and high quality products, which they believe are only found outside of China, specifically in Western countries (*China Economic Times*, 2014). *Economic Observer* reported similar motivations among entrepreneurs: "As early as eight years ago he [Li Wentao] and his family had become Canadian green cards holders. 'Immigrating can provide a better future for my children,' said Li Wentao" (Tang Xiangyang and Cao Xingbi, 2013).

Yet another prominent motivation for emigration is related to China's lack of legal institutionalization, particularly the lack of private property rights and endemic corruption, and their consequence—a growing sense of insecurity (specifically related to assets and property) that has spread throughout China's entrepreneurial class. China's wealthy entrepreneurs have articulated their concerns over China's unfavorable political climate and have cited this as a reason for emigration. For example, a leader of China's real estate industry referenced the now infamous Bo Xilai affair as an example of this state predation against China's entrepreneurs, and in referencing this event, noted that a Bo Xilai governed China would have all but guaranteed a mass exodus of these entrepreneurs (Wang, 2013). Indeed, according to one media report, many entrepreneurs fled China in the wake of the "crackdown on illegal activities" by Chongqing authorities, a campaign which was eventually exposed for its true intentions: targeting entrepreneurs and their capital (Ma Guochuan, 2014). As one report states, the three wealthiest entrepreneurs in Chongqing—Peng Zhimin, Li Jun and Chenming Liang—were included in those arrested; their property was seized and their families destroyed. As a result, "some entrepreneurs have begun to transfer their private property overseas, or simply emigrate overseas (at that time more than 200 entrepreneurs emigrated to Canada)" (Ma Guochuan, 2014).

Indeed, Tong Zhiwei, a professor at East China Normal University, published a paper that claimed that the real purpose of the crackdown in Chongqing was to target the private sector, specifically by dismantling private enterprises and seizing private property, the capital of which was then channeled to local administrations and SOEs (Ma Guochuan, 2014). Persistent worry over private property has indeed grown unabated. According to a *China Economic Times* report, inadequate property law and property rights has caused a severe degree of anxiety among China's entrepreneurial class, especially the rich, and as a result, the especially wealthy entrepreneurs have either already emigrated out of China entirely or are contemplating doing so (2014).

Various surveys of entrepreneurs have also reinforced the argument that entrepreneurs are increasingly unquiet over China's lack of property rights protections, and as a result, some have embraced the move to emigrate as one response to this problem. *Economic Observer*, which conducted a two-month-long investigation to assess how secure entrepreneurs feel, found that:

> 42.86 percent of entrepreneurs are currently experiencing extreme anxiety; an additional 35.71 percent of entrepreneurs are mildly anxious; and only 1.43 percent of entrepreneurs believe they are without anxiety. . . . There are many reasons which explain this anxiety. Hardships and difficulties associated with engaging in business, fierce competition, and worsening of the market environment all can be seen as reasons. Nevertheless, the most common phrase mentioned by entrepreneurs when surveyed about this topic was insecurity (Tang Xiangyang and Cao Xingbi, 2013).

Furthermore, "40 percent of the surveyed entrepreneurs revealed that the current business environment is 'not beneficial to competition' " and that "small and medium enterprises clearly are even more vulnerable" (Tang Xiangyang and Cao Xingbi, 2013).

Specific examples of Chinese entrepreneurs, and their comments, further support these findings. For example, the tragic circumstances of Chinese entrepreneur Ceng Chengjie and his encounter with the state have given the entrepreneurial community further reason to feel vexed. Ceng Chengjie, who was charged with "investment fraud," was subsequently executed by the state, while his family was left in the dark on the situation. *Sina Finance* reported that, as a result, the entrepreneurial community feels the "government's violation of property rights has become a phenomenon," marked first by its expropriation, and followed by its redistribution to government entities, all with the blessing of the courts (Ma Guochuan, 2014). Jiang Likuan, an entrepreneur who attempted entrepreneurial ventures on three different occasions, touched upon a related point in the following excerpt that is integral not only to the healthy functioning of a market economy but also to the entrepreneurs that fuel its growth—knowing the rules of the game in advance. As he noted, "When doing business one should understand the rules, but much of the time a clear understanding of the rules is absent. They are always changing." He also said that an unpredictable and inadequate legal environment is one of the biggest obstacles to entrepreneurship (Tang Xiangyang and Cao Xingbi, 2013).

Yan Jun, Lu Tianyu, and Zhou Pu, three entrepreneurs also surveyed by *Economic Observer*, similarly spoke out about this particular problem, noting that the legal ambiguity that pervades entrepreneurial and economic activities, specifically the predictability required for the successful creation of enterprises and for day-to-day operational management, has caused great anxiety among entrepreneurs, and has restricted competition and growth. Yan Jun, who owns a water service company and is based in Beijing, openly conveyed the severe ambiguities surrounding China's economic and legal environment; Lu Tianyu, who owns an Internet company, conveyed a similar sentiment, stating that the environment is "unpredictable" and "nothing is clear"; and Zhou Pu expressed how he is always on edge and feels enormous pressure (Tang Xiangyang and Cao Xingbi, 2013).

As a result of this precarious legal framework, entrepreneurs have expressed that they must tread ever so carefully in their relations with the government in general, and officials in particular, the management of which has exacted a great toll on the daily—and ultimately future—success of their businesses. Li Wentao, Lu Tianyu, and Teng Binsheng, provided personal accounts of their struggle over what constitutes appropriate interactions and healthy relations with government. Li Wentao, for example, explained how he knows very well to keep his distance from the government. Lu Tianyu went even further and said that for entrepreneurs, the further away from officials you are the better off you will be. These views represent nearly 43 percent of entrepreneurs surveyed. Another entrepreneur, Teng Binsheng even said that this game that is played between entrepreneur and official creates a heavy burden for entrepreneurs. Nearly 43 percent said they want an environment more conducive to conduct business and nearly 39 percent said the law needs to be strengthened, especially to protect private property (Tang Xiangyang and Cao Xingbi, 2013).

Yet, evidence indicates that the desire to emigrate is likely confined to those entrepreneurs who have amassed great fortunes, and thus who are a relatively small fraction of the millions of entrepreneurs now operating within China. Moreover, two distinguishing features of these entrepreneurs, who have decided to emigrate, seems to be both their age and family size: both age—born before or well before 1980—and whether or not one has children seem to weigh heavily in an entrepreneur's decision to emigrate, or remain in China, as the aforementioned Li Wentao demonstrates (Tang Xiangyang and Cao Xingbi, 2013). Furthermore, out of the entrepreneurs the author interviewed, there was no indication that any given entrepreneur had a desire to emigrate, nor did these entrepreneurs allude to an emigrating trend among their ranks (i.e., among the *Baling Hou* generation of entrepreneurs operating small to medium sized businesses).

On the contrary, these *Baling Hou* entrepreneurs feel tightly connected to this new and constantly transforming reform-era China, and through discussions with the author expressed a desire to remain in China and make their own contributions toward improving the environments in which they live and conduct business. As one entrepreneur noted:

> Most of them like the Western countries—that is democracies, and democratic values. Half of them believe China has a very bright future, on the rise and I am one of them. There is another smaller half that think—I'm going to set up a business, make a lot of money, and then maybe go to America, Europe, Australia, because in their business experience they have dealt with corruption and they don't want their kids dealing with these issues (Entrepreneur 16).

Indeed, during the interviews multiple references were made to a new and emerging mentality among this new generation of entrepreneurs, one that valued more than money and wealth, particularly one that made a lasting impact on the positive development of China, whether it be the economic, social, or political sphere. Some were more general but identified this perspective and trend: "These people [the *Baling Hou* generation of entrepreneurs] speak more freely and their ways of thinking are slightly different. But what I think is important is that they also need to realize that they are special and willing not only to make money, but also willing to do something good to make the country's future a little bit better" (Entrepreneur 7).

China's Internet Mediums: a Vehicle for Class Organization and Political Voice?

The advent and proliferation of Internet mediums has served as a vehicle for the creation of a critical public sphere and to showcase dissenting views. Indeed, as one survey revealed, the increasing levels of political participation are being facilitated by advancements in technology (particularly the Internet), which make participation both less laborious and less costly than in previous periods (Wang Junxiu, 2006, 72). The Internet in China, which as of 2008 had 235 million registered users (ZSH, 2011, 304), has also helped facilitate a critical sphere, where members can engage in politicized discussion with less fear of being targeted for political infractions. As one article notes in the analysis of public opinion over the Internet, "Chinese netizens display a consistent sense of intense social concern, and the Internet has become an important public opinion channel for all circles to express their interests and feelings, and to exchange thoughts" (ZSH, 2011, 303). Themes of discussion include "a sense of justice, an earnest search for the truth, and sympathy for the vulnerable" (ZSH, 2011, 311). Finally, the *Baling Hou* generation represents a majority of Internet users. According to a study by the China Internet Information Center, "68.6 percent of total Chinese netizens" were "30 years old and below" (ZSH, 2011, 304–305).

Furthermore, these emerging Internet mediums have not only facilitated a critical cyber sphere, but moreover, they have begun to replace traditional forms of information gathering: according to the China Internet Information Center, "Over 80 percent of netizens mainly depended on the Internet to gain their news, exceeding the importance of television as well as newspapers and periodicals" (ZSH, 2011, 305). This reveals not only the declining ability of the state in using these mediums for propagating its ideology but also in providing an objective source for China's citizens to gather information. As one article noted: "With the overall size of Internet traffic doubling every 5 years or so, digital media usage now routinely nurtures the spirit of monitory democracy . . . helped by sophisticated proxies and other methods of avoiding censorship, salacious tales of official malfeasance circulate fast, and in huge numbers" (Keane, 2012). Guthrie echoes this thought, recounting cases where Chinese officials attempted to limit the spread of information over the Internet and were ultimately unsuccessful, concluding that it has become "a new frontier for outright resistance" (Guthrie, 2006, 275). A *South China Morning Post* article noted an increase in protests in a five-year period, and the significance of the Internet in facilitating this growth:

> The party's policy has been to isolate such protests and contain any attempts at larger scale organization. This strategy, however, is becoming increasingly difficult. The digital culture—the internet, in particular weibo, and mobile phone cameras—is tearing down boundaries in time and space. In the past two years, the number of microbloggers went from few to more than 300 million. A convergence between what's happening off and on line seems inevitable (Ljunggren, 2012).

Another report portrayed precisely how Internet communication is providing an accountability mechanism for society in their quest to check official (including family members) abuse and their attempts to be above the law. In one case, "Internet users revealed that the 15-year old son of a general was one of two young men who crashed a BMW into another car in Beijing and then beat up its occupants, warning onlookers not to call police. An uproar ensued, and the general's son has now been sent to a police correctional facility for a year, state media report" (Page, 2011).

The Internet in general, and microblogs such as weibo in particular, serve as powerful mechanisms and vehicles through which the entrepreneurial class pursues its interests and attempts to realize its values. For example, in what began as the party's praise for the revolutionary party chief Bo Xilai and his apparent crackdown on organized crime, not only turned against him with details that incriminate him in acts of extortion, bribery and arbitrary interrogation that have led to his detention, but as a result, China has witnessed one of the largest instances of societal discussion and organization via the Internet. Furthermore, the discussion centered on the criticism of the party to the point where the party intervened and implemented a freeze on the use of microblogs: "the government clampdown has prompted some prominent internet users to speak out, with some of the strongest criticism coming from influential businessmen" (Chao, 2012). As one businessman stated, "In order to prevent the spreading of rumors, they shut down the comment function but left the repost function open. Is that the right medicine for the illness?." According to the article, "his post had been reposted more than 8,000 times by Sunday" (Chao, 2012). An interview with Zhang Xin, a Chinese entrepreneur, further supported the notion of the online world as a growing force in conjunction with generational change in China. At one point in the interview she stated the following:

> I think that China will face major challenges in the near term. With every generation of leaders, the power base has become weaker and weaker. When you go on the Chinese blogs, you will see how little credibility the Chinese government has among the Chinese people. I think this will be the major challenge. How do you address a country where the governing power is losing the trust of the people? (Murray, 2011).

An article in China's *Nanfang Zhoumo* (*Southern Weekly*) illustrated the power of weibo as a vehicle for the transmission of information, particularly information related to political policy and political views. Although some entrepreneurs do invariably participate in formal political institutions, such as the NPC and CPPCC, the article noted that the discussions on weibo are more effective and have a greater reach. For example, just before the NPC and CPPCC meetings in 2013, a Chinese businessman "posted a Two Sessions weibo message which was subsequently reposted over 30,000 times. Individuals who helped repost the message included entrepreneurs with influential social media accounts such as Pan Shiyi, Xu Xiaoping [founder of ZhenFund], and Xue Manzi." Another businessman also posted on weibo, which was "reposted nearly 20,000 times." Indeed, as the article notes, "these 'chit-chats' on the Internet . . . have a profound and far-reaching influence and have become another prospect for entrepreneurs' political discussions" (Chenzhong Xiaolu, 2013).

As mentioned earlier, Xi Jinping has sought to wrest greater control over Internet activity in general and Internet activity that criticizes the party, in particular. This has taken the form of "technological upgrades" to "prevent undesirable content from entering and circulating," formulating "new laws and regulations," and "aggressively punishing those who defy the new restrictions" (Economy, 2018, 58–59). Indeed, one news article posited that under Xi, many different forms of Internet discussion and expression, including commenting on current events and CCP members, now lead to arrests, and that this complete disregard for the rule of law is even reminiscent of Mao's GPCR (Voice of America, 2013).

Although navigating and utilizing the Internet for organizational and political purposes may be more challenging in the Xi Jinping era, this hasn't stopped netizens from taking to the Internet to project their voices. For example, three years into Xi's reign, netizens took to the Internet to publicize that a group of women were arrested for their attempt to protest. Netizens not only utilized popular Chinese social media applications, but also other more secure portals to carry out and organize online discussion. The CCPs attempts to quell these netizens appeared futile; the women became known internationally, which generated more online discussion and even street protests. This case alone appears to show that netizens aren't afraid to express their voices, despite Xi's suppressive regulations, and are adept at finding solutions to the CCPs attempted censorship of Internet activity (Economy, 2018, 84–85). In yet another example, also three years into Xi's reign, netizens took to the Internet to express their anger over a chemical explosion at a warehouse, which resulted in a substantial number of injuries and even deaths. Netizen activity, including posting and viewing comments, proliferated widely within just days following the incident (Economy, 2018, 88–89).

China's attempt to exert greater party control over the Internet and to suppress certain Internet activity also comes at an economic cost to the party, which, in turn, has the potential to further frustrate the entrepreneurial class and produce sociopolitical consequences. By suppression and limiting exchange and expression online, the party deprives the Chinese people of a "shared sense of community" and "creative expression," and negatively affects the economy (Economy, 2018, 59). Indeed as Economy writes, "many Chinese businesspeople and academics argue that the loss of access to VPNs limit their ability to be innovative" (2018, 85–86). Ultimately, by taking this action, the party effectively further frustrates society, in general, and the entrepreneurial class, in particular, and suppresses economic growth, both of which the party desperately needs—on its side—to retain its legitimacy (derived from continued economic growth) and its claim to a monopoly on political power.

The author's interviews with entrepreneurs substantiated the utility of the Internet in facilitating discussion and organizational agency within this emerging private sphere. An interview the author conducted with an entrepreneur in May 2012 exemplifies the growing use of platforms such as weibo as a result of dissatisfaction with the one-party system. This particular entrepreneur had recently established a business designed to fill a growing demand in

China: that of access to safe and quality food. Although the business allows for convenient shopping—via physical devices in home or online apps, as well as delivery—its inspiration resulted from the growing issues of food safety in China, and the entrepreneur's overall passion for responding to what he terms the party-related "bugs" in contemporary China (Entrepreneur 18).

Indeed, during our discussion this particular interviewee regularly returned to this term the "bugs" in contemporary China. What was significant about this reference was not simply his understanding of China's predatory environment, but his statement that weibo has provided the means for individuals such as himself to remain comprised of current events, including access to real-time information on party-related abuses. His examples included the Sichuan earthquake, explaining how weibo exposed the party's misappropriation of funds, which were donated specifically to the government-established earthquake fund for the families of victims, but where "70 percent of the funds went to Beijing's central authorities, and only 30 percent went to Sichuan Province of which a large percentage went to constructing extravagant villas for party-officials"; and the uncovering of why one school was destroyed while the neighboring school stood unaffected: it was funded by a private donor who personally saw to the oversight of the construction, while the one destroyed fell victim to what is all too common in contemporary China—compromised construction while lining the pockets of officials (Entrepreneur 18). As he noted:

> In China we have government departments to check food safety, but they are doing nothing. Every timc they will wait for the complaints; if they don't complain they will still sell and the trouble will continue. Even if customers complain they still won't do anything. The reason why this came to the fore in the Carrefour issue [the early 2012 case where Carrefour sold contaminated fish] because it affected a famous star who posted this on weibo. . . . In China we cannot rely on government related institutions for food safety checks. The government institutions capitalize on profiteering (奸商) and thus allow poor safety standards to continue (Entrepreneur 18).

Additional interviews indicate a similar finding—that of the link between weibo and government exposure and de-legitimization of the one-party system. In response to the question, "Do you think that China will retain a single party system for a long time?," one particular entrepreneur replied, "That is their dream, but after the invention of Twitter I don't know for how long" (Entrepreneur 14). Following the completion of our interview, she asked if she could continue further discussing the issue of contention between growing entrepreneurial forces and the lack of political institutional change. As our discussion proceeded, the author explained to her the case he observed while living in Beijing during the 2008 Olympics: that of the universal absence of knives from store shelves in Beijing; immediately following the completion of the Olympics, knives immediately reappeared. In response to this, and in continuing our discussion on Internet vehicles, communication and organization, she stated:

> The government has so much fear. And also the other thing is . . . there was an article on Chinese Twitter about how to control the people in Germany. One of the guys responsible for this broadcast on Twitter listed 8 points—how to fool the people. This is exactly what the Chinese government is using right now. But with the Internet and Twitter, they cannot fool the people anymore. A couple of days ago I recalled in my mind that Chairman Mao was a tall guy because we always believe if you are powerful then you are tall and handsome, and therefore, we always believed that he was 1.83 meters tall. But do you know what happened? He was only 1.72 meters tall. The broadcast system tried to fool the people (Entrepreneur 14).

Furthermore, this particular interviewee perceived the importance of online communication, such as Twitter, and its implications for China's political future, particularly considering the amount of state predation she has experienced and observed in China. When the author asked her "How long will China's predatory environment continue?," she stated:

> Until we change the one party system. Otherwise we will never have hope. But since the intervention of the Internet, and in China Twitter was allowed to run, we get a lot more information. It is impossible for the government to try and prevent us from acquiring information. And because of this I believe big changes will come here soon for the government. Either themselves or they will be changed by the people in China. They have created a lot of anger in this country. People hate the rich guys, and hate those who have power . . . rich guys here are rich because they screw people, because they have relationships, because they are doing some illegal dirty business, but are protected by the government officers. It is dangerous now (Entrepreneur 14).

As a result of these clashes and subsequent entrepreneurial disaffection with China's legal and political apparatus, the entrepreneurial class is increasing its politicized discussion on the Internet—not to mention extending this to face-to-face organized discussion. Many of the entrepreneurs the author interviewed indicated the link between Internet vehicles such as weibo, and political discussions and entrepreneurial empowerment. As one commented: "Normally we talk about these things on the Internet; we want to fix the bugs stemming from the government. . . . People are becoming more empowered on weibo. In fact the younger generation, with voices that are rights-conscious and expressive, are increasing" (Entrepreneur 18).

Finally, although political demonstrations are still an exception, entrepreneurial gatherings—at entrepreneurs' businesses, at entrepreneurial forums, and cafés—to hold discussions, including political discussions, seems to be an increasing norm, as indicated in interviews with several entrepreneurs. During one particular interview, when asked "As a result of China's modernization, do you feel that a new mentality has emerged in China's entrepreneurs?," the entrepreneur highlighted how his generation (this particular entrepreneur was 27 years old) not only gathers to hold discussions, but no longer holds them in the traditional manner:

> Now the young generation goes to coffee places. We don't need a round table with 10 or twelve people all having big dinners so that we can start up a discussion. Many of these people either have a government background or are older. But for people like me I would like to invite people here to my business to talk and have coffee or tea. In fact this is happening with those business owners that have not had overseas experiences. Many *haigui* are very similar. We prefer to be at coffee shops or businesses, and we help each other with business discussions. But I think people are slowly willing to accept this way. My dad for example, who is in his 50s is even starting to switch to café environments (Entrepreneur 7).

In another example, a Shanghai-based entrepreneur, who originated from Chengdu, specifically made the comment that Chinese entrepreneurs—though still in a nascent stage—are beginning to discuss political issues more freely and prevalently. Although according to her much of the political discussion is still on a micro level, there is evidence of group-based political discussions: she made it clear that she discusses political issues on a regular basis with her friends, and sometimes in large groups. She also noted that the rise of Internet mediums has markedly facilitated this development (Entrepreneur 15):

> Yes—some friends and I discuss these issues on a regular basis. Weibo—Chinese twitter—is where many entrepreneurs express their personal opinions, through this platform, on social and political issues. Many times we talk about the bigger picture in China—the social and political issues. The younger generation are definitely much more open to discussing these things. The older generation has—PTSD—post-traumatic stress disorder—they are afraid to talk about it. But the younger generation are not. They are looking for freedom, and to take action on this freedom. But I don't think it has really formed a community, it is still more individual-based. The mainstream maybe is still more concentrated on personal issues—not the big picture (Entrepreneur 15).

Furthermore, at one point in the interview she stated: "One time I was at an event and asked a question—no one could answer. Someone told me after that they appreciated my question, except for the fact that no one could answer it. I told her that when I ask a question, the point isn't always to get an immediate answer, but instead, to generate discussion and further thought" (Entrepreneur 15).

In November 2011 the author attended an all-day annual entrepreneurial forum in Shanghai that resembled a collaborative entrepreneurial environment (mostly those of the *Baling Hou* generation). The event was centered on entrepreneurial pitches in the form of approximately thirty-minute presentations and discussions. In fact, one of the entrepreneurs interviewed was a leading figure at this entrepreneurial forum, and gave a speech in the afternoon presenting his business platform, including the concepts behind his innovative business as well as imminent plans to expand. Most noteworthy, are the following points he made regarding the fundamental concept of his business—to encourage entrepreneurial collaboration and unity: "The purpose of my business: not just coffee and a seat; and equally not just people and a seat. But furthermore, the purpose is to 1) get people connected; 2) get them talking; 3) and 'break the cubicle' mentality" (Entrepreneur 7). This entrepreneur later informed the author that he was finishing construction of his second location—another start-up incubator, housing entrepreneurs with ideas but those still without resources to develop these ideas. The size of the first location is 100 square meters; the second is four times the original location—400 square meters. Finally, in a recent follow-up discussion with this entrepreneur, he mentioned that political discussion within the startups at his business is common (Entrepreneur 7).

Thus, China's entrepreneurial class has demonstrated a deep understanding of China's rule by law-driven endemic corruption, based on their regular clashes with it, and are articulating the source of the problem and how to resolve it. The consequence of this development for the party has been the slow erosion of its legitimacy and rising frustration within the very social forces fueling China's economic growth, something the party has attempted with great tenacity to prevent since its decision to reform and open up in 1978. China's entrepreneurs have shown a desire to discuss this core problem, and political solutions to it, at cafés, at their businesses, and through the Internet, among other means. Evidence suggests the emergence of an entrepreneurial class, particularly *Baling Hou* entrepreneurs, that is increasingly embracing liberal political values, while also beginning to organize around—and for—these values in order to secure their fundamental rights and freedoms. Indeed, some entrepreneurs have even articulated how political change would take place and that China's entrepreneurs would be the harbingers of this change.

Several responses from different entrepreneurs reveal how they envision this process taking shape. As one entrepreneur noted in an interview:

> It is all connected. It starts with the economy, and then the little business owners will become really big, and then there will be more and more businessmen

> who will be chosen as government representatives from this group, and then they will already have the power to speak and advise, and that is how they will improve the conditions for their business, and is how they will influence the government later. The businessmen will be the representatives of the people when they get to this position, and into the government. They have money, then they have social alliance, so they have power. I hope I have the same future. I want to change China at this level. I want to see Chinese people living not just surviving (Entrepreneur 9).

In a separate interview in spring 2012 an entrepreneur responded by saying: "I would say that entrepreneurs will be the main contributor to political change because I can't think of any other class of people who will be motivated to do that, or have that kind of mentality or even power to do that. They (other classes) just want to follow what other people do, right?; entrepreneurs are supposed to be troublemakers—I know, I am a troublemaker" (Entrepreneur 17). Finally, in a separate interview, the entrepreneur projected entrepreneurial-driven political change: "I think if anyone is going to drive political change, it will be from the entrepreneurial class" (Entrepreneur 17).

Thus, at least a portion of China's entrepreneurs are demonstrating that they are on the brink of full liberal maturation, articulating specific political requirements to ensure property protections and a predictable operating environment, and organizing and acting in support of these values. Consequently when—not whether—entrepreneurial-driven political institutional change will occur seems to increasingly be the relevant question (see Figure 6.1).

CONCLUSION

As established in the previous chapter, China's entrepreneurial class operates under a rule-by-law system that, based on their personal experiences, has produced predatory behavior (official malfeasance and organizational corruption) and an unpredictable legal environment; the question is, how have—and how will—China's entrepreneurs respond to this unfavorable environment? Particularly how have the *Baling Hou* generation responded, and how will their response(s) evolve moving forward? This chapter demonstrated that the majority of entrepreneurs are disinterested in a conservative solution to their problem, that is, wedding with the party through party membership, bribery of local officials, or other expenditures, and by doing so theoretically reaping benefits and immunities. Indeed, survey data and interviews reveal that the

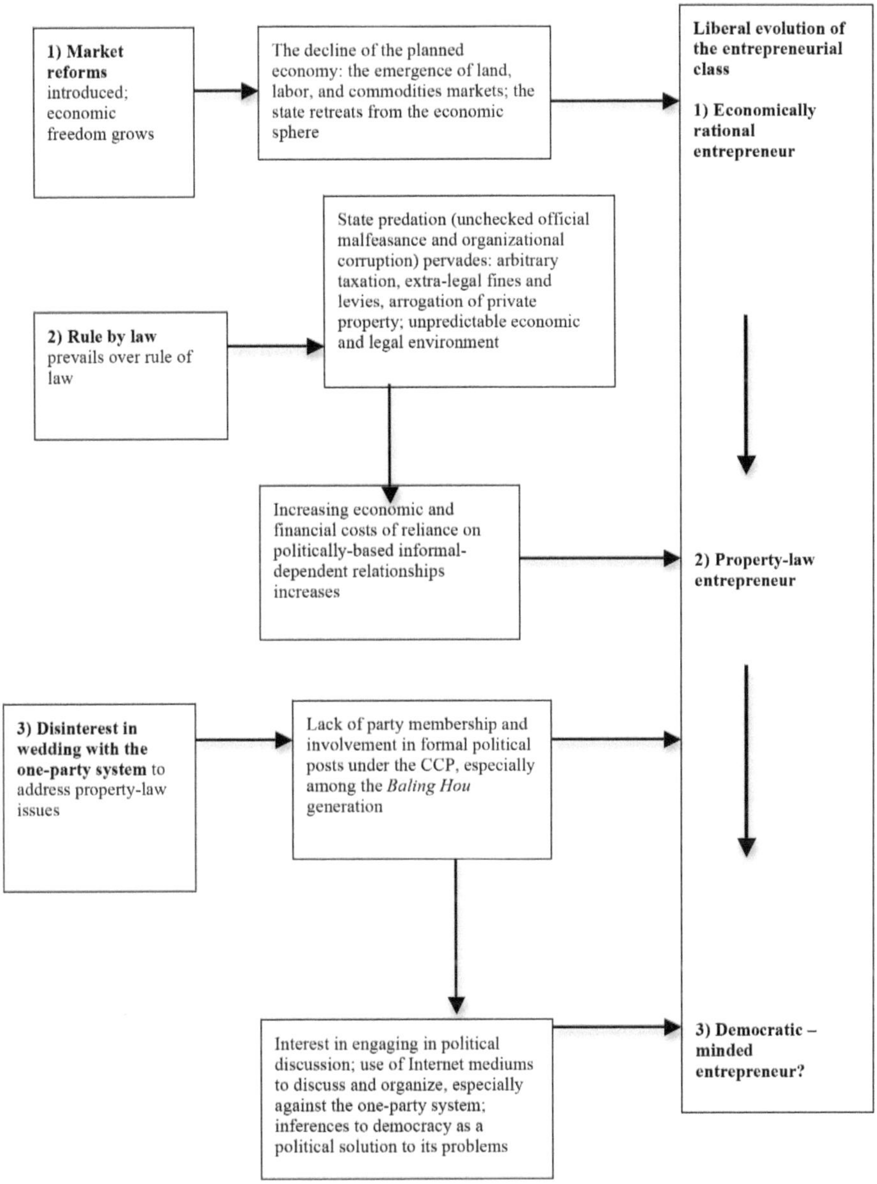

Figure 6.1. Causal Modeling of Liberal Development in Contemporary China
Figure produced by the author

majority of entrepreneurs with party membership were party members prior to diving into entrepreneurship, and there is little interest among the *Baling Hou* generation to acquire this once essential status. Furthermore, the majority of entrepreneurs also seem to be disinterested in emigrating out of China for the purpose of resolving this fundamental dilemma.

Instead, China's entrepreneurs seem motivated to seek alternative internal solutions to their problem by pursuing internal institutional change, with some even touching on the need for democracy. China's entrepreneurs in general and the *Baling Hou* in particular are articulating a desire for greater political awareness and an interest in engaging in political discussions among peers especially as it pertains to China's legal system and business environment. Many are utilizing online mediums to express their individual and class interests, even if politically sensitive and in opposition to the party. To be sure, entrepreneurial-driven, substantive political-institutional change, is unlikely to be imminent, but unless the party decides to crush this class, which is unlikely considering that the party's legitimacy hinges on continued economic success, they will continue to grow in size and force. Thus, at this point the relevant question here seems to be a quantitative one—when will the entrepreneurial class be in a position to substantively challenge the party—rather than a qualitative one—whether they will fully evolve into a liberal class vying for liberal political values: the rule of law and political input and participation.

Chapter Seven

Conclusion

Prospects for a Contemporary Chinese Bourgeoisie

England's socioeconomic development highlights the evolution of liberalism and how it evolved to produce a liberal entrepreneurial class capable of inducing political institution change. England's particular conditions—relatively weak absolutist institutions, strong markets, intractable peasant protests, and ultimately a revenue crisis for the landowning classes—incentivized a break from feudalism and an embrace of capitalism. This shift toward markets, and greater efficiency and innovation, also created the rational and enterprising entrepreneur, and provided the economic foundation from which England would experience a fundamental social-structural, and ultimately political-institutional, transformation. This increasingly individualist and property-oriented class highlighted the fundamental contradiction that exists when a rule by law and closed political system governs over a market economy and the drivers of economic growth—the entrepreneurial class. The more the state enacted prohibitive taxation and threatened private property, and resisted political reforms, the more the entrepreneurial class solidified and organized around its property-law interests. The result was the evolution of the third and final phase of its trajectory, that is, a class not only with interests, and organized around these interests, but one that recognized the need for substantive political institutional change to ensure their protection.

China's socioeconomic trajectory, on the other hand, diverged from that of England. Prior to reform and opening in 1978, China made three attempts at modernization, most visible during the Song dynasty and the Republican and Maoist eras, each of which ended short of full liberal maturation. China began its economic ascent centuries before England, yet managed to level off and enter a period of economic stasis before it had a chance to see subsequent transformations of its social structure and ultimately political institutions. China's limited experience with feudalism, and the widespread existence of independent farming and even land ownership, especially by the Song dynasty, catapulted China into a period of unprecedented growth. Markets grew, efficiency and specialization increased, and innovation and technological achievements proliferated. Yet two central features of China's experience—the civil service exams which culled people into the bureaucracy and provided security and wealth, and a lack of incentive to mechanize and industrialize—perpetuated the economic status quo. Furthermore, China's levels of taxation were relatively low and its mode of governance was such that it limited antagonism and opposition from below. Thus, economic stasis beget social-structural stasis, which coupled with the lack of a predatory state, resulted in stalled liberal growth after reaching its first phase—that of a liberal class in the economic sense of the term, a rational entrepreneurial class.

A glimmer of liberalism emerged during the Republican era, yet, instability, militarism, and the rise of the CCP and the consolidation of its power would ultimately ensure the extinction of liberalism. Liberal entrepreneurial elements did emerge in the first part of the twentieth century; indeed they were economically rational and autonomous, aware of the importance of the rule of law for property protection, with some even embracing liberal political values. Yet, they were limited to the coastal regions, particularly Shanghai, and due to widespread political instability, including endemic warlordism and militarism, were unable to extend their paradigm. The CCP's rise to power would ensure, through a series of campaigns spanning decades, the liquidation of all remaining liberal elements. Mao effectively crushed the entrepreneurial class and the private sector, and with it, any hope for a new Chinese liberalism.

China's post-1978 shift in economic policy, as well as important political-institutional reforms, have created the possibility for the revival of a liberal entrepreneurial class and the emergence of a new Chinese liberalism. Some people had hoped—indeed believed—that early on China's economic reforms and subsequent economic growth would produce fundamental changes to China's social class structure and ultimately to its political institutions. The latter, of course, has yet to happen. Nevertheless, China's fundamental contradiction—a *rule by law* authoritarian regime governing over a transforming social class structure in which a property-owning entrepreneurial class is expanding—grows by the day, and, the author would argue, at the party's own peril. Seemingly unmoved by this danger, Xi Jinping has, in unprecedented fashion, reverted to a leadership style akin to the Maoist era, exemplified in his decision to abolish one of Deng Xiaoping's signature political-institutional reforms—term limits; in his attempts to suppress Internet activity political in nature; and most recently in his decision to expand China's United Front work (China's attempt to "co-opt and neutralize sources of potential opposition to the policies and authority of its ruling Chinese Communist Party") by establishing two additional bureaus to include new areas, one of which "targets representatives of the 'New Social Classes,' [and] is responsible for garnering support from China's new middle class" (Bowe, 2018, 4). Indeed, Xi's decision to expand China's United Front apparatus harkens back to Jiang Zemin's historic speech eighteen years earlier, which sought to co-opt—and by extension neutralize—private entrepreneurs. As detailed in chapter 6, attempts to co-opt entrepreneurs should prove increasingly futile; and strengthening the party's authoritarian tendencies will likely jeopardize Xi's leadership if not the party as a whole.

Two developments in China since 1978—the emergence of a new generation of entrepreneurs born after 1980 and the growing contradiction of a one-party *rule by law* state overseeing market reforms and economic freedom—have created the conditions which make possible social opposition to China's political status quo and a push for political-institutional change. China's *Baling Hou* entrepreneurs possess a very different mentality than that of their predecessors who lived during Mao's reign or even prior to 1949: the idea of unswerving loyalty to the party, the center, and the leader are lost on this group; instead, they possess a mentality that emphasizes the individual. This fundamental distinction has provided a foundation that has led them on a very different trajectory—whether it be the realm of economics, jurisprudence, or politics. Thus, they are an important component—indeed addition—to China's ongoing economic—and potentially political—transformation.

The author's interviews with China's emerging entrepreneurial class identified the existence of a rational and autonomous class—a liberal class in the economic sense of the term. China's private entrepreneurs in general and the *Baling Hou* generation in particular have indicated strong support for China's newfound market economy and sphere of economic freedom, including newfound access to lucrative opportunities that allow for aggregation of capital and wealth. They resemble China's entrepreneurs of the Republican Era—the Nanyang Brothers, Y. Moh and C. C. Nieh—who spearheaded the unprecedented growth of Chinese industry to fill the demands of emerging markets. China's new private entrepreneurs are harbingers of innovation and advancement and in a wide range of spheres: mobile apps, advertising, business incubators and online services, to name a few. Indeed, many entrepreneurs have even left their positions, many with healthy salaries, to capitalize on opportunities in emerging markets, and to risk an uncertain future for the potential rewards that attend entrepreneurship.

China's entrepreneurs have also become increasingly independent-minded, and along with it, detached from the party's absolute ideology and its claim to dogmatic truths. Entrepreneurs have noted the differences between their parents' generation and their own, in particular, the amount of freedom they are afforded and the consequences of this freedom in fostering a new philosophy, most notably one characterized by individual autonomy. Furthermore, many entrepreneurs made reference to the ways in which the party has attempted to manage the formation of new ideas and maintain ideological superiority over them, such as the use of the formal education system or the media. Notwithstanding, entrepreneurs have indicated their growing immunity to party ideology, thus potentially paving the way for a new philosophy based upon individual rights and freedoms—a bourgeois philosophy in the legal and political sense of the term.

The author's interviews with entrepreneurs, in addition to the wealth of surveys and reports on China's pervasive corruption and state predation, also point to an entrepreneurial class aware of China's grossly insufficient legal system and possessing property-law interests. China's newfound sphere of economic freedom has brought widespread acquisition of property, which, coupled with China's *rule by law*, has produced an entrepreneurial class recognizing and calling for property protections. A perennial theme among entrepreneurs during the author's interviews was constant frustration over pervasive and egregious official malfeasance—including arbitrary levies, arrogation of property, and arbitrary notices and policies. Entrepreneurs have been forced to pay arbitrary fines after establishing their businesses; compelled to find new locations for businesses after months of planning, due to unexpected and arbitrary reversals of initial approvals; forced to purchase superfluous equipment to pay taxes; and even find their businesses arbitrarily shut down for periods of time, to name a few. In response, some entrepreneurs have resorted to wining and dining local officialdom, gift-giving, and bribes, but many conveyed that these measures necessarily increase over time and are ultimately unsustainable.

China's fundamental contradiction—that of an authoritarian *rule by law* one-party state overseeing market reforms, a sphere of economic freedom, and a growing class of entrepreneurs—continues unabated, which has forced China's entrepreneurs to consider whether they wish to continue wedding with the party, which would include party membership, bribes, gift-giving, and taking up formal political posts; or diverge from the party and advocate for the *rule of law*. Based on the author's interviews and a review of survey data, China's entrepreneurs appear overwhelmingly disinterested in continuing to expend vast sums of resources to keep local officialdom at bay and their businesses operating, and are equally disinterested in party membership; instead, they have indicated a desire to move further toward the *rule of law* to protect their property and interests, including improvements to the "control, supervision and execution" (Entrepreneur 12) of the law and constitutional amendments to protect private property.

China's entrepreneurs have also demonstrated a degree of political liberalness, indicating the possibility for the emergence of a bourgeoisie. For one, they are politically aware, as many entrepreneurs interviewed indicated their interest to stay informed of political developments. Furthermore, not only did interviews reveal that entrepreneurs are overwhelmingly disinterested in party membership (not a single interviewee was a party member, nor did any have a desire to join the party; and although party membership was desired in previous generations, in their generation in general, and within the entrepreneurial class in particular, the desire for party affiliation and state involvement is limited), but a review of survey data also confirmed this trend. Despite Jiang Zemin's call in 2001 for entrepreneurs to join the party and use their productive activities to contribute to the party and its future, entrepreneurs remained unmoved and disinterested in party membership. China's entrepreneurs are also showing signs of organization around the values that define their newfound philosophy in a way that evokes the development of the critical-political public sphere in the evolution of the Western bourgeoisie, while utilizing modern advanced Internet technologies to voice their concerns and opinions. Indeed, the case of Wukan, where viral discussions and protests forced the party to concede to the voice of society, and where the implementation of local elections was the outcome; the Bo Xilai affair, where entrepreneurs' comments were censored by the party; and even examples of continued use of the Internet in the era of Xi Jinping, particularly social media, to express one's voice and organize against party abuses, demonstrate an increasing desire among social elements, including the entrepreneurial class, to expose the party's rule by law governance and question the current political system.

Moreover, entrepreneurs do not seem to be entertaining the idea of exiting China as a solution to their politico-legal problems, with the exception of the particularly wealthy entrepreneurs discussed in chapter 6. Instead, they seem intent on remaining in China and continuing with their business activities, while conscious of the serious juridical problems they face and solutions to them. One particular entrepreneur, for example, stated that "the one-party system" is the problem (Entrepreneur 14). Indeed, several entrepreneurs interviewed said that future political reform or change will likely be initiated by the entrepreneurial class, and some even went as far as saying that "democratic political reform" or "democratization" (Entrepreneur 10) will be the type of change (Entrepreneur 9, 17).

Thus, although many have discarded the notion of a liberal entrepreneurial class and have equally discarded a Chinese path toward the liberal liberation of its people, this project has identified an emergent entrepreneurial class with potential for political maturation into a bourgeoisie. With the accelerated growth of the entrepreneurial class beginning in the early 1990s, and the evolution of liberal characteristics—economically rational, property-law interests, political awareness and an understanding of the need for political institutional change, and political agency—catalyzed by engagement with markets, the acquisition of private property, and a predatory state, the foundation for the emergence of a new Chinese liberalism is being set. As a consequence, the formation of a class for itself, a bourgeoisie, is becoming more likely in China.

Ultimately, there appears to be three roads forward for China and the CCP. The first is to maintain the status quo: promote a market economy and economic growth, and allow the existence of an entrepreneurial class and economic freedom, but resist genuine legal and political institutional change. As previously mentioned, this presents a fundamental contradiction: the continuation of a rule by law single-party authoritarian system that governs over the continued growth of a private sector and entrepreneurial class that has growing demands for the rule of law. This contradiction requires resolution, at some point, and is not a sustainable path forward. The second is to embrace a style of governance akin to Maoist China: suppress the private sector, give prominence to state control of the economy and ownership of enterprises and property, and ultimately crush the entrepreneurial class. This, also, is not a viable option, at least if the party wishes to survive. To crush the entrepreneurial class would be to also end the party's one source of legitimacy—economic growth—and to draw the ire of its own officials who support reforms and have benefited from them. The third path forward is for the CPP to cede to, or be taken over by, the wishes and interests of an emergent entrepreneurial class, including its demands for the rule of law and necessary political change, particularly representation. This appears to be the only plausible outcome. The unprecedented revival of China's private entrepreneurial class, beginning in 1978, and accelerated in the 1990s, is, as time moves on, increasingly likely to produce the emergence of a new Chinese liberalism and fundamental, entrepreneurial-driven, political institutional change.

Appendix

Interview Questions

PART 1: ECONOMIC FREEDOM

What do you do for a living? How would you define your position in Chinese society?
您目前以什么为生？您觉得您目前在中国社会中:处于什么样的阶层（位置)?

If I can ask, what did your parents do for a living? How does your life differ from theirs?
您父母以什么为生？您的生活和您父母有什么不同？

How do you feel about China's new market economy and new societal wealth? Do you think that China has a class system like that in Western countries?
您对中国的市场经济和社会财富程度怎么看？您觉得中国目前是否存在着和西方国家类似的阶级？

Do you think that China will have a "middle-class society" such as exists in the West?
您觉得中国会变成类似西方目前存在的中产阶级社会吗？

As a result of China's modernization, do you feel that a new mentality has emerged in China's entrepreneurs? Explain.
鉴于中国的现代化，您觉得在中国的私营企业主阶层中出现了一种新的思路或心理吗？请解释。

PART 2: PRIVATE PROPERTY AND THE RULE OF LAW

How many people work in your business?
您公司/企业有多少员工？

Do you feel there are any factors which prevent you from maximizing on economic ventures and acquiring wealth?
您觉得目前有没有一些因素影响到了您扩大经营规模和盈利？

Is it better to increase the size of your business, or remain small? Why?
您觉得扩大生意规模对您是否是一个很好的选择？还是保持现状？为什么？

What is your understanding of private property? Does private property exist in China?
您对私人财产是如何理解的？私人财产在中国是否存在？

Do you feel that China's legal system adequately protects your property? Do you think private property protection and the rule of law have been strengthened in the recent period?
您认为中国的法律是否能够足够保护您的财产？您认为在最近一段时期私人财产的保护和法律规则是否得到加强？

What is your view on corruption in China? Do you feel a need for the rule of law in order to limit corruption and protect your property?
你怎样看待中国腐败现象？你认为依法治国可以遏制腐败和保护你的财产吗？

Is it possible to effectively administer the rule of law inside a single party system? If not, what is the solution?
您认为在一党制的系统下，法律规章制度是否可能有效地进行管理？如果
不是，您认为有什么解决办法？

PART 3: POLITICAL LIFE

How would you characterize the relationship between your business and the government? Do you have good and beneficial relations; or are there some issues?
您如何描述您的生意/业务和政府之间的关系？是不是一个良好且有益的关系？或者是否还有一些其他方面的事情（关系/因素）？

Are you interested in China's politics? Do you think businesspeople should take an interest in politics; or is it best to keep politics and business separate?
您对中国政治感兴趣吗？您觉得商人是否应该对政治感兴趣？还是最好将政治和经商
分开？

Are you involved in the CCP? What is the purpose of your involvement in the CCP?
您是中国共产党党员么？您加入中国共产党的目的是什么？

Do you think that China will retain a single party system for a long time? What is your impression of the views of business-people on this matter?
您觉得中国是否会在很长一段时间内保持一党制？您从商人的角度是如何看待这个问题
的？

Do you think the government will introduce direct elections for people's congresses? Would you support this move now; and what is your impression of the views of businesspeople on this question?
您觉得中国人大会采取直选的方式吗？您会支持这个变革吗？从商人的角度是如何看待这个问题的？

Do you discuss politics with other business members? How much political discussion do you see among the businesspeople?
你是否和其他商会成员讨论政治?据你观察商人当中讨论政治的比例是多少?

What is the future of China's entrepreneurs?
中国私营企业主阶层的未来是什么？

References

Anderson, P. (2013) *Lineages of the Absolutist State.* New York: Verso.

Ao Daiya (2005) "Siying Qiyezhu Zhengzhi Canyu Yanjiu Baogao [Research Report on the Political Participation of Private Entrepreneurs]," in Zhang Houyi, Hou Guangming, and Li Mingzhi (eds.) *Zhongguo Siying Qiye Fazhan Baogao* [Report on the Development of Private Entrepreneurs in China]. Beijing: Shehui Kexue Wenxian Chubanshe, pp. 61–83.

Areddy, J. (2011) "China Report Harsh on Rail Push," *The Wall Street Journal, Asia (hereafter, WSJ, Asia),* 29 December, (VOL. XXXVI No. 85), p. 3.

Atsushi, S. (1984) "The Origins and Structure of Gentry Rule," in Grove, L. and Daniels, C. (eds.) *State and Society in China: Japanese Perspectives on Ming-Qing Social and Economic History*. Tokyo: Tokyo University Press, pgs 335–385.

Barboza, D. (2011) "Entrepreneur's Rival in China: The State," *The New York Times,* 7 December. Available at: http://www.nytimes.com/2011/12/08/business/an-entrepeneurs-rival-in-china-the-state.html?pagewanted=all

Barnett, D. A. (1964) *Communist China, The Early Years: 1949–1955.* New York: Praeger.

Baum, R. (1994) *Burying Mao: Chinese Politics in the Age of Deng Xiaoping.* Princeton: Princeton University Press.

BBC News (2010) "Eight Held After Deadly Shanghai High-rise Blaze," 16 November. Available at: https://www.bbc.com/news/world-asia-pacific-11762817

BBC News (2011) "China Bullet Train Crash 'Caused by Design Flaws,'" 28 December. Available at: http://www.bbc.co.uk/news/world-asia-china-16345592

BBC News (2012) "China Overturns Death Sentence of Entrepreneur Wu Ying in Fraud Case," 20 April. Available at: https://www.bbc.com/news/world-asia-china-17787189

Becker, J. (1996) *Hungry Ghosts: Mao's Secret Famine.* New York: Henry Holt.

Bergère, M-C. (1983) "The Chinese Bourgeoisie: 1911–1937," in Fairbank, J. and Twitchett D. (ed.) *The Cambridge History of China: Republican China, 1912–1949, V. 12,* pp. 722–826.

Bergère, M-C. (1989) *The Golden Age of the Chinese Bourgeoisie: 1911–1937.* Cambridge: Cambridge University Press.

Bergère, M-C. (2009) *Shanghai: China's Gateway to Modernity.* Stanford: Stanford University Press.

Bowe, A. (2018) *China's Overseas United Front Work: Background and Implications for the United States.* Washington, D.C.: U.S.-China Economic and Security Review Commission.

Brandt, L., Ma, D., and Rawski, T. (2014) "From Divergence to Convergence: Reevaluating the History Behind China's Economic Boom," *Journal of Economic Literature,* 52(1): pp. 45–123.

Brenner, R. (1985) "Agrarian Class Structure and Economic Development," in T.H. Aston and C.H.E. Philpin (eds.) *The Brenner Debate: Agrarian Class Structure and Economic Development in Pre–Industrial Europe.* Cambridge: Cambridge University Press, pp. 10–63.

Brenner, R. (1985b) "The Agrarian Roots of European Capitalism," in T.H. Aston and C.H.E. Philpin (eds.) *The Brenner Debate: Agrarian Class Structure and Economic Development in Pre–Industrial Europe.* Cambridge: Cambridge University Press, pp. 213–327.

Brenner, R. (1993) *Merchants and Revolution: Commercial Change, Political Conflict, and London's Overseas Traders, 1550–1653.* Princeton: Princeton University Press.

Brook, T. (1999) *The Confusions of Pleasure: Commerce and Culture in Ming China.* Berkeley: University of California Press.

Calhoun, C. (1997) *Neither Gods Nor Emperors: Students and the Struggle for Democracy in China.* Los Angeles: UC Press.

Chaffee, John W. (1986) *The Thorny Gates of Learning in Sung China.* Cambridge: CUP.

Chang, C. L. (1962) *The Income of the Chinese Gentry.* Seattle: University of Washington Press.

Chang, G. (2012) "Chinese Entrepreneurs are Leaving China," *Forbes*. Available at: http://www.forbes.com/sites/gordonchang/2011/06/05/chinese-entrepreneurs-are-leaving-china/2/ (Accessed 24 January).

Chang, M. H. (2002) *Falun Gong: The End of Days.* New Haven: Yale University Press.

Chao, L. (2012) "China Curbs Web Commentary," *WSJ, Asia,* 02 April. (VOL XXXVI No. 149), p. 4.

Chen, Theodore Hsi-En and Chen, Wen-hui C. (1953) "The 'Three-Anti' and 'Five-Anti' Movements in Communist China," *Pacific Affairs,* 26(1): pp. 3–23.

Chen Guangjin (2002) "Siying Qiye Zhu de Shehui Laiyuan, Jieceng Yishi yu Zhengzhi—Shehui Canyu Fenxi [Analysis of the Social Origins, Class Mentality and Political Participation of China's Private Entrepreneurs]," in Zhang Houyi, Ming Lizhi, and Liang Zhuanyuan (eds.) *Zhongguo Siying Qiye Fazhan Baogao* [Report on the Development of China's Private Entrepreneurs]. Beijing: Shehui Kexue Wenxian Chubanshe, pp. 27–85.

Cheng Li (2010) "Chinese Scholarship on the Middle Class: From Social Stratification to Political Potential," in Cheng Li (ed.) *China's Emerging Middle Class: Beyond Economic Transformation.* Washington, D.C.: Brookings Institution Press, pp. 55–83.

Chenzhong Xiaolu (2013) "Entrepreneurs' Political Discussions [Qiyejia Yizheng]," *Nanfang Zhoumo*, 14 March. Accessed at: http://www.apabi.com.

Chen, S. K. (1914) *The System of Taxation in China in the Tsing Dynasty*, 1644–1911. New York: Columbia University Press.

Choi Chi-Yuk (2012b) "Wang Lijun's Successor Rises Through the Ranks," *SCMP*, 30 March. http://www.scmp.com/portal/site/SCMP/menuitem.2af62ecb329d3d773 3492d 9253a0a0a0/?vgnextoid=b10028cd12f56310VgnVCM100000360a0a0aR CRD &ss=China&s=News

Chou En-lai (1959) "China Greets Soviet Party Congress: Chou En-lai's Speech," *Peking Review*, 3 February (5), pp. 6–9.

Chu, T. T. (1988) *Local Government in China Under the Ch'ing.* Cambridge: Harvard University Press.

Coble, P. (1979) "The KMT Regime and the Shanghai Capitalists," *China Quarterly*, 77(March): pp. 1–24.

Cooper, J.P. (1985) "In Search of Agrarian Capitalism," in T.H. Aston and C.H.E. Philpin (eds.) *The Brenner Debate: Agrarian Class Structure and Economic Development in Pre–Industrial Europe.* Cambridge: Cambridge University Press, pp. 138–191.

Croot, P and Parker, D. (1985) "Agrarian Class Structure and the Development of Capitalism: France and England Compared" in Aston, T. H. and Philpin, C. H. E. (eds.) *The Brenner Debate: Agrarian Class Structure and Economic Development in Pre-Industrial Europe*. Cambridge, MA: Cambridge University Press, pp 79–90.

Dali Yang (2004) *Remaking the Chinese Leviathan: Market Transition and the Politics of Governance in China*. Stanford: SUP, pp. 217–258.

Deng Xiaoping (1980) "TV Interview with Deng Xiaoping," *Peking Review*, 14 January (2), pp. 18–23.

Deng Xiaoping (1994) *Selected Works of Deng Xiaoping: 1982–1992, V. 3.* Beijing: Foreign Languages Press.

Dickson, B. (2003) *Red Capitalists in China: The Chinese Communist Party, Private Entrepreneurs, and Political Change.* Cambridge: Cambridge University Press.

Dickson, B. (2008) *Wealth into Power: The Communist Party's Embrace of China's Private Sector.* Cambridge: Cambridge University Press.

Dickson, B. (2010) *Allies of the State: Private Entrepreneurs and Democratic Change.* Cambridge: Harvard University Press.

Dong Liu (2016) "Fangzhi Yin Banan Budang Daozhi "Anjian Banle, Qiye Kuale," [Avoiding the "Collapse of Enterprises" Due to the Mishandling of Legal Cases], 03 March. Available at www.atabi.com. 1960.

Economy, E. (2018) *The Third Revolution: Xi Jinping and the New Chinese State.* New York: Oxford University Press.

Ebrey, P. (2010) *The Cambridge Illustrated History of China*. Cambridge: Cambridge University Press.

Elvin, M (1973) *The Pattern of the Chinese Past*. Stanford: Stanford University Press.

Encausse, H. C. and Schram, S. (1969) *Marxism and Asia.* London: Allen Lane.

Fairbank, J. (1986) *The Great Chinese Revolution 1800–1985*. New York: Harper-Perennial.

Fiol-Mahon, A (2018) "Xi Jinping's Anti-Corruption Campaign: The Hidden Motives of a Modern-Day Mao," *Foreign Policy Research Institute*. Available at: https://www.fpri.org/article/2018/08/xi-jinpings-anti-corruption-campaign-the-hidden-motives-of-a-modern-day-mao/

Gamester, N. (2011) *The Legatum Institute Survey of Entrepreneurs: China 2011*. London.

Gardner, J. (1969) "The *Wu–fan* Campaign in Shanghai: A Study in the Consolidation of Urban Control," in Bennett, D. (ed.) *Chinese Communist Politics in Action.* Seattle: University of Washington Press, pp 477–539.

Genser, J. and Cohen, J. (2012) "Harmful Effects," *SCMP,* 26 January. http://www.scmp.com/portal/site/SCMP/menuitem.2af62ecb329d3d7733492d 9253a0a0a0/?vgnextoid=7285d4f5fa415310VgnVCM100000360a0a0aRCRD &ss=China &s=News.

Goldman, M. (1994) *Sowing the Seeds of Democracy in China: Political Reform in the Deng Xiaoping Era.* Cambridge: Harvard University Press.

Guthrie, D. (2006) *China and Globalization: the Social, Economic and Political Transformation of Chinese Society.*New York: Routledge.

Gu Jianjian (2006) "Dangqian Siyingqiyezhu Jieceng Guanzhu de Wenti" [The Problems that the Entrepreneurial Class is Most Closely Following], *Beijing Ribao*, 28 August. Available at: www. Apabi.com. 1750

Habermas, J. (1989) *The Structural Transformation of the Public Sphere: An Inquiry into a Category of Bourgeois Society.* Cambridge: MIT Press.

Harding, H. (1987) *China's Second Revolution: Reform after Mao.* Washington, D.C.: Brooking Institution Press.

Harding, H. (1991) "The Chinese State in Crisis," in Twitchett, D and Fairbank, K. (eds.) *The Cambridge History of China, V. 15.* Cambridge: Cambridge University Press, pp. 107–217.

Hegel, G.W.F. (1952) *The Philosophy of Right, the Philosophy of History.* Chicago: Encyclopedia Britannica.

Hegel, G.W.F. (1995) *Lectures on Natural Right and Political Science: The First Philosophy of Right, Heidelberg 1817–1818 with Additions from the Lectures of 1818–1819.* Transcribed by Peter Wannenmann; Edited by the Staff of the Hegel Archives; Translated by J. Michael Stewart and Peter C. Hodgson. Berkeley: University of California Press.

Hilton, R. H. (1985) "A Crisis of Feudalism," in T.H. Aston and C.H.E. Philpin (eds.) *The Brenner Debate: Agrarian Class Structure and Economic Development in Pre–Industrial Europe.* Cambridge: Cambridge University Press, pp. 119–137.

Ho, P. (1954) "The Salt Merchants of Yang-Chou: A Study of Commercial Capitalism in Eighteenth-Century China," *Harvard Journal of Asiatic Studies*, 17(1/2): pp. 130–168.

Holt, R. and Turner, J. (1966) *The Political Basis of Economic Development*. Princeton: Van Nostrand Company.

Hu Jintao (2012) "Adhering to the Socialist Cultural Development Path with Chinese Characteristics and Striving to Build a Country with a Strong Socialist Culture," *Qiu Shi*, 1 January (4)1. Available at: http://english.qstheory.cn/magazine/201201/201203/t20120331_149043.htm

Huanqiu Shibao (2011) "Qiyejia Mingyun yu Zhonggong Jinmi Xianglian" [The Fates of the Entrepreneurs and the Chinese Communist Party are Inseparably Linked], 22 June, p. 15.

Huang, P. (1990) *The Peasant Family in Rural Development.* Stanford: Stanford University Press.

Ji Beibei (2012) "Carrefour Faces Food Scandal," *Global Times,* 19 April. Available at: http://www.globaltimes.cn/NEWS/tabid/99/ID/705795/Carrefour-faces-food-scandal.aspx.

Jiang Zemin (2001) "Speech at the Meeting Celebrating the 80th Anniversary of the Founding of the CPC," *Beijing Review,* 29(July 19): pp. i–xvi. Jiao, P. (2011) "Railway Official Owns 'US$1m Villa'," *SCMP.* 21 December. Available at: http://archive.scmp.com/showarticles.php.

Jiao, P. (2011) "Railway Official Owns 'US$1m Villa'", SCMP. 21 December. Available at: http://archive.scmp.com/showarticles.php.

Jing Huang (2008) "Institutionalization of Political Succession in China: Progress and Implications," in Cheng Li (ed.) *China's Changing Political Landscape: Prospects for Democracy.* New York: Brookings Institution Press, pp. 80–97.

Jing Lin and Xiaoyan Sun (2010) "Higher Education and China's Middle Class," in Cheng Li (ed.) *China's Changing Political Landscape: Prospects for Democracy.* New York: Brookings Institution Press, pp. 217–242.

Keane, (2012) "The China Labyrinth," *SCMP.* 20 February. Available at: http://www.scmp.com/portal/site/SCMP/template.printACopy/page.scmp_prin tacopy/vgnextoid=68b5e01d06595310VgnVCM100000360a0a0aRCRD

Lardy, N. (1987) "Economic Recovery and the 1st Five-Year Plan," in Twitchett, D. and Fairbank, K. (eds.) *The Cambridge History of China, V. 14.* Cambridge: Cambridge University Press, pp. 144–184.

Lardy, N. (2019) *The State Strikes Back.* Washington, D.C.: Peterson Institute for International Economics.

Lee, M. (2011) "Chinese Writers Slam Baidu for Copyright Infringement," 16 March. Available at: http://www.reuters.com/article/2011/03/16/us-baidu-copyright-idUSTRE72F2QJ20110316.

Lefebvre, G. (2005) *The Coming of the French Revolution.* Princeton: Princeton University Press.

Lerner, D. (1958) *The Passing of Traditional Society: Modernizing the Middle East.* London: The Free Press.

Levy, M. J. Jr. (1949) "The Social Background of Modern Business Development in China," in *The Rise of the Modern Chinese Business Class: Two Introductory Essays.* New York: International Secretariat, pp. 2–17.

Lin Chun (2006) *The Transformation of Chinese Socialism.* Durham, NC: Duke University Press.

Lipset, S. M. (1959) "Some Social Requisites of Democracy," in *American Political Science Review*, 53(1): pp. 69–105.

Lipson, E. (1920) *An Introduction to the Economic History of England.* London: A. & C. Black.

Liu Shao-ch'i (1958) "Document 25: Liu Shao-ch'i, *The Present Situation, the Party's General Line for Socialist Construction and its Future Tasks,* May 5,

1958," in The Joint Auspices of the Center for International Affairs and the East Asian Research Center, Harvard University (1962, ed.) *Communist China, 1955–1959: Policy Documents with Analysis.* Cambridge: Harvard University Press, pp. 416–438.

Liu Shao-ch'i (1969) *Collected Works of Liu Shao–ch'i, 1945–1957.* Hong Kong: Union Research Institute.

Ljunggren, B. (2012) "System Tests," *SCMP,* 27 January. http://www.scmp.com/portal/site/SCMP/menuitem.2af62ecb329d3d7733492d9253a0a0a0/?vgnextoid=f3a811cd3e915310VgnVCM100000360a0a0aRCRD&ss=China&s=News

Ma Guochuan (2014) "Qiyejia zhe Shi Nian: Qiye Mingyun zai Dangzheng Huiyishi bei Jueding" [Entrepreneurs in the Past Ten Years: The Fate of Enterprises is Decided in Party and Government Conference Rooms], *Xinlang Caijing* [Sina Finance], 14 April. Available at http://finance.sina.com.cn/china/20140414/094118788164.shtml

Macfarlane, A. (1978) The *Origins of English Individualism: the Family, Property, and the Social Transition.* New York: Cambridge: University Press.

MacFarquhar, R. (1974) *The Origins of the Cultural Revolution, V. 1.* Oxford: Oxford University Press.

MacFarquhar, R. (1983) *The Origins of the Cultural Revolution, V. 2.* Oxford: Oxford University Press.

MacFarquhar, R. (1997) *The Origins of the Cultural Revolution, V. 3.* Oxford: Oxford University Press.

Magnier, M. (2004) "The State Taketh, Chinese Entrepreneurs Say," *Los Angeles Times,* 11 March. Available at: http://articles.latimes.com/2004/mar/11/world/fg-owners11.

Malik, R. (1997) *Chinese Entrepreneurs in the Economic Development of China.* Westport: Praeger.

Mann, S. (1987) *Local Merchants and the Chinese Bureaucracy, 1750–1950.* Stanford: Stanford University Press.

Mao Zedong (1951) "Comments on the Work of Suppressing and Liquidating Counterrevolutionaries," in (1974, ed.) *Miscellany of Mao Zedong Thought, 1949–1968.* Arlington: Joint Publications Research Service, pp. 6–8.

Mao Zedong (1952) "Directive on the Five-Anti Movement," in (1974, ed.) *Miscellany of Mao Zedong Thought, 1949–1968.* Arlington: Joint Publications Research Service, p. 11.

Mao Zedong (1954) *Selected Works of Mao Zedong, Volume I.* London: Lawrence and Wishart LTD, pp. 13–20.

Mao Zedong (1969) *Selected Works, Volume IV.* Peking: Foreign Languages Press.

Mao Zedong (1977) *Selected Works, Volume V.* Peking: Foreign Languages Press.

Martin, J. (1983) *Feudalism to Capitalism: Peasant and Landlord in English Agrarian Development.* Palgrave.

Marx, K. (1926) *The Eighteenth Brumaire of Louis Bonaparte.* London: Allen and Unwin.

Marx, K. (1936) *The Poverty of Philosophy.* London: M Lawrence Limited.

McGregor, R. (2010) *The Party: The Secret World of China's Communist Rulers.* London: Allen Lane.

Mio Kishimoto (2011) "Property Rights in Imperial China," in Debin Ma and Jan van Luiten Zanden (ed.) *Law and Long–Term Economic Change: A Eurasian Perspective*. Stanford: SUP, pp. 68–90.

Moore, B. Jr. (1966) *Social Origins of Dictatorship and Democracy. Lord and Peasant in the Making of the Modern World.* London: Penguin Press.

Moore, B. (1989) "Liberal Prospects Under Soviet Socialism," at *The First Annual W. Averell Harriman Lecture, November 15.* The W. Averell Harriman Institute for Advanced Study of the Soviet Union: Columbia University.

Murray, A. (2011) "China has Politics, Too: Why 2013 May be the Perfect Time to Engage the Chinese in Constructive Dialogue," *WSJ, Asia,* November 21, 2011, R5; R11.

Nef, J. (1968) *Industry and Government in France and England, 1540–1640.* New York: Russell & Russell.

Ng Tzewei (2012b) "Death is too High a Price for Wu to Pay," *SCMP,* 02 February. Available at: http://www.scmp.com/portal/site/SCMP/menuitem.2af62ecb329d3d7733492d9253a0a0a0/?vgnextoid=65a5111960935310VgnVCM100000360a0a0aRCRD&ss=China&s=News

The *North China Herald* (1916a) "Chinese Press, Dr. Wu Ting-Fang's Advice," 5 May (VOL CXVIII): p. 251.

The *North China Herald* (1916b) "The Coming Conference at Nanking, Peking, May 9," 20 May (VOL CXVIII): p. 376.

The *North China Herald* (1916c) "Chinese Press, The Chiangchun of Hunan, May 16," 20 May (VOL CXVIII): p. 377.

The *North China Herald* (1916d) "The Shanghai Markets: Piece Goods," 20 May (VOL CXVIII): p. 402.

The North China Herald (1916e) "China's Foreign Trade in 1915, May 23," 27 May (VOL CXVIII): pp. 426–427.

The *North China Herald* (1919a) "China's Old Man of the Sea, Dec. 31," 4 January (CXXXIII): p. 5.

The *North China Herald* (1919b) "Rise of Chinese Cotton Mills: Important Development in Local Spinning," 30 August (CXXXII): p. 550.

The *North China Herald* (1919c) "Rise of Chinese Cotton Mills: A Change in Old Ideas," 30 August (CXXXII): p. 550.

The *North China Herald* (1919d) "Rise of Chinese Cotton Mills: Chinese Surpassing Japanese," 30 August (CXXXII): p. 551.

The *North China Herald* (1919e) "The China Assocn. Meeting, Sept 26," 27 September (CXXXII): p. 784.

The *North China Herald* (1921) "A Chinese Merchant on China's Sorrows: Striking Speech by Dr. F. C. Tong: Coming to Grips with the Real Difficulties of China: Eloquent Appeal to Business Men to Face Facts and Act," 15 October.

Page, J. (2011) "Children of the Revolution," *WSJ, Asia,* 26 November. https://www.wsj.com/articles/SB10001424053111904491704576572552793150470

Page, J. and Spegele B. (2011) "Beijing Set to Strike Hard at Revolt," *WSJ,* 16 December. Available at: https://www.wsj.com/articles/SB10001424052970204026804577100132882903066

Page, J. (2012a) "China's Rich Weigh Moving to U.S, Europe," *WSJ, Asia,* 23 February, (VOL XXXVI No. 122), p. 14.

Page, J. (2012b) "Chongqing Party Chief Intrigue Thickens," *WSJ, Asia,* 09 March, (VOL XXXVI No. 133), p. 4.

Page, J. (2012c) "Unfolding Scandal Clouds Chinese Party Chief's Ascent," *WSJ, Asia,* 12 March, (VOL XXXVI No. 134), p. 4.

Page, J. (2012d) "Two Chiefs' Style Make for China Congress Buzz," *WSJ, Asia,* 02– 04 March, (VOL XXXVI No. 128), p. 1; 6.

Page, J. (2012e) "Dead Briton Worked on Intelligence," *WSJ, Asia*, 27 March, (VOL XXXVI No. 145), p. 6.

Peking Review (1965) "Welcoming 1966—The First Year of China's Third Five-Year Plan," 1 January (1): pp. 5–9.

Peking Review (1968) "Great Cultural Revolution in Progress: The Army and People Pledge to Fulfil the Militant Tasks for 1968," 12 January (2): pp. 8–9.

Peking Review (1978) "Communiqué of the Third Plenary Session of the 11th Central Committee of the Communist Party of China," 52 (December 29): pp. 6–16.

Peking Review (1980a) "Communiqué of the Fifth Plenary Session of the 11th Central Committee of the Communist Party of China," 10 March (10), pp. 7–10.

Peking Review (1980b) "Resolution on Establishing the Secretariat of the Central Committee," 10 March (10), pp. 3; 11–17.

Polanyi, R. (1957) *The Great Transformation: the Social and Economic Origins Our Time.* Boston: Beacon.

Pu Xingzu (1987) "Increase the Authority of Legislative Bodies," *Chinese Law and Government,* 20(1): pp. 78–83.

Renmin Ribao (1979) "Jiaqiang Fazhi Fayang Renmin Cujin Sihua" [Strengthen the Legal System and Carry on with the Four Modernizations], 5 July, p. 1–2; FBIS, 10 July, pp. L3–L7.

Reuschemeyer, D., Stephens, E., and Stephens, J. (1992) *Capitalist Development and Democracy.* Cambridge: Polity Press.

Root, H. (1994) *The Fountain of Privilege: Political Foundations of Markets in Old Regime France and England.* Berkeley: University of California Press.

Rosen, S. (2009) "Contemporary Chinese Youth and the State," *The Journal of Asian Studies* 68(2): pp. 359–369.

Shi Jiangtao (2012) "Closed Doors to Reform," *SCMP,* 30 January. Available at: http://www.scmp.com/portal/site/SCMP/menuitem.2af62ecb329d3d7733492d9253a0a0a0/?vgnextoid=ccac5f5af6925310VgnVCM100000360a0a0RCRD&ss=China&s=News

Skocpol, T. (1979) *States and Social Revolutions: A Comparative Analysis of France, Russia and China.* Cambridge: Cambridge University Press.

Solinger, D. (1993) *China's Transition from Socialism: Statist Legacies and Market Reforms, 1980–1990.* Armonk: M. E. Sharpe.

Spegele, B. (2012b) "Wukan Vote Tests China Waters," *WSJ, Asia,* 02 February, (VOL XXXVI No. 107).

Stavis, B. (1987) "Editor's Introduction," *Chinese Law and Government,* 20(1): pp. 3–14.

Strand, D. (1989) *Rickshaw Beijing: City People and Politics in the 1920s.* Berkeley: University of California Press.

Tan Jian (1987) "Reform and Strengthen China's Political System," *Chinese Law and Government.* 20(1): pp. 44–50.

Tang Xiangyang and Cao Xingbi (2013) "Caifu de Jilu" [Wealth's Anxieties], *Jingji Guangcha Wang* [Economic Watch Online]. 12 October. Available at http://www.eeo.com.cn/2013/1012/250667.shtml.

Tawney, R. H. (1912) *The Agrarian Problem in the Sixteenth Century.* London: Longman Greens and Co.

Teiwes, F. (1987) "Establishment and Consolidation of the New Regime," in Twitchett, D and Fairbank, K. (eds.) *The Cambridge History of China, V. 14.* Cambridge: Cambridge University Press, pp. 51–143.

Teiwes, F. (1993) "The Establishment and Consolidation of the New Regime, 1949–1957," in Macfarquhar, R. (ed.) *The Politics of China: 1949–1989.* Cambridge: Cambridge University Press, pp 6–86. Tien, M. (2012) "Safety off the Rails," *SCMP,* 6 January. Available at: http://archive.scmp.com/showarticles.php.

Tombs, R. (2014) *The British and Their History.* Cambridge, MA: Cambridge University Press.

Transparency International (2012–2019) "Corruption Perceptions Index." Available at: https://www.transparency.org/research/cpi/overview

Tsai, K. (2007) *Capitalism Without Democracy: the Private Sector in Contemporary Sector.* New York: Cornell University Press.

Tsou, T. (1991) "The Tiananmen Tragedy: "the State-Society Relationship, Choices, and Mechanisms in Historical Perspective," in Womack, B. (ed.) *Contemporary Chinese Politics in Historical Perspective.* Cambridge: CUP, pp. 265–327.

Tung Ta-Lin (1959) "A Socialist Industrial Army for Agriculture," *Peking Review,* 20 January (3), pp. 6–9.

Voice of America (2013) "World Media Watches China: Bizarre Repression." Available at: https://www.voachinese.com/a/world-press-china-20131010/1767050.html

Von Glahn, R. (2016) *The Economic History of China: From Antiquity to the Nineteenth Century.* Cambridge: Cambridge University Press.

The *Wall Street Journal*, Asia, (2012) "China's New Cultural Revolution," 04 January, (VOL XXXVI No. 88), p. 9.

The *Wall Street Journal*, Asia, (2012a) "Hong Kong Struggle Sessions," 11 January, (VOL XXXVI No. 93), p. 9.

The *Wall Street Journal*, Asia, (2012b) "China's Local Tyrants," 28 March, (VOL XXXVI No. 146), p. 11.

Wang Junxiu (2006) "*Dangqian Zhongguo Shehui Xintai Fenxi Baogao* [An Analytical Report of China's Current Social Psychology]," in Ru Xin, Lu Xueyi, and Li Peilin (eds.) *2006 Nian: Zhongguo Shehui Xingshi Fenxi yu yu ce* [Analysis and Forecast of China's Social Development]. Beijing: Shehui Kexue Wenxian Chubanshe, pp. 67–81.

Wang, S. (2011) "Ex Cadre Jailed after Years of Corruption," *SCMP,* 18 December. Available at: http://archive.scmp.com/showarticles.php.

Wang Yan (2010) "Recipe for a Fulfilling Career," *China Daily,* November 9, p. 2.
Wang, Z. (2013) "Why China's New Rich Want to Emigrate," *The Diplomat*, November 05.
Wei Haibo (1987) "Reform of the Political System and Political Democratization," *Chinese Law and Government* 20(1): pp. 74–77. Y
Wen-hui Tsai (1983) *Patterns of Political Elite Mobility in Modern China, 1912–1949.* San Francisco: Chinese Materials Center.
Wen-hui Tsai (1986) "From Traditional Modernity: A Socio-Historical Interpretation on China's Struggle Towards Modernization Since the Mid-19th Century," *Reprint Series in Contemporary Asian Study Series*, 1(72).
White, G., Howell, J. and Shang, X. (1996) *In Search of Civil Society: Market Reform and Social Change in Contemporary China.* New York: Oxford University Press.
Whyte, M. K. (1991) "Urban Life in the People's Republic," in MacFarquhar, R. and Fairbank, K. (eds.) *The Cambridge History of China, V. 15.* Cambridge: Cambridge University Press, pp. 682–742.
Wong, R. Bin (1997) *China Transformed: Historical Change and the Limits of European Experience.* Ithaca: Cornell University Press.
Wong, R. Bin and Rosenthal, Jean-Laurent (2011) *Before and Beyond Divergence: The Politics of Economic Change in China and Europe.* Cambridge: Harvard University Press.
Wong, R. Bin (2012) "Taxation and Good Governance in China, 1500–1914," in Bartolome, Y.C., O'Brien, P. and Comin Comin, F. (eds.) *The Rise of Fiscal States, A Global History 1500–1914.* Cambridge: Cambridge University Press, pp. 353–377.
Xiaobo Lü (2000) *Cadres and Corruption: The Organizational Involution of the Chinese Communist Party*. Stanford: Stanford University Press.
Xu Zhaoming (1987) "The Changing Function of the Government in the Transformation of China," *Chinese Law and Government* 20(1): pp. 26–34.
Xue Muqiao (1980) "On Reforming the Economic Management System," *Peking Review,* 4 February (5), pp. 16–21.
Yan, A. (2012) "Lawyer Who Takes Price in Picking Hard Battles," *SCMP,* 12 February. Available at: http://www.scmp.com/portal/site/SCMP/menuitem.2af62ecb329d3d7733492d 9253a0a0a0/?vgnextoid=29e1750371d65310VgnVCM100000360a0a0aRCR D&ss=China&s=News
Yiyi Lu (2011) "China's Privileged Rule-Breakers," *WSJ, Asia.* Available at: http://blogs.wsj.com/chinarealtime/2011/05/27/chinas-privileged-rule-breakers/.
Yu Ran (2011) "Officials Jailed Over Shanghai Inferno," *China Daily*, 08 March. Available at: http://www.chinadaily.com.cn/cndy/2011– 08/03/content_13037086 .htm.
Zagorin, P. (1959) "The Social Interpretation of the English Revolution," *The Journal of Economic History,* 19(3): pp. 376–401.
Zhai, K. (2012) "Resurrecting Comrade Lei Feng," *SCMP*, 04 March. Available at: http://www.scmp.com/portal/site/SCMP/menuitem.2af62ecb329d3d7733492d 9253a0a0a0/?vgnextoid=656564659a8d5310VgnVCM100000360a0a0aRCR D&ss=China&s=News

Zhang, E. (2012) "Nations Small Traders Squeezed Dry," *SCMP,* 20 January. http://www.scmp.com/portal/site/SCMP/template.printACopy/page.scmp_printacopy/vgnextoid=dd95a0120f5f4310VgnVCM100000360a0a0aRCRD.

Zhang Houyi (1999) "Siying Qiye Zhu de Qunti Tezheng [Group Characteristics of China's Private Entrepreneurs]," in Zhang Houyi and Ming Lizhi (eds.) *Zhongguo Siying Qiye Fazhan Baogao* [Report on the Development of China's Private Entrepreneurs]. Beijing: Shehui Kexue Wenxian Chubanshe, pp. 227–297.

Zhang Houyi (2004) "Jinru Xin Shiqi de Zhongguo Siying Qiye Zhu Jiceng [A New Period for China's Private Entrepreneurial Class]," in Ru Xin, Lu Xueyi, and Li Peilin (eds.) *2004 Nian: Zhongguo Shehui Xingshi Fenxi yu yu ce* [Analysis and Forecast of China's Social Development]. Beijing: Shehui Kexue Wenxian Chubanshe, pp. 311–320.

Zhang Houyi (2005) "Kuaisu Chengzhang de Zhongguo Siying Qiye Zhu Jieceng [The High-Speed Growth of China's Private Entrepreneurs]," in Ru Xin, Lu Xueyi, and Li Peilin (eds.) *2005 Nian: Zhongguo Shehui Xingshi Fenxi yu yu ce* [Analysis and Forecast of China's Social Development]. Beijing: Shehui Kexue Wenxian Chubanshe, pp. 328–338.

Zhang Houyi (2006) "A New Phase in the Development of the Status of Private Entrepreneurs," in *The China Society Yearbook: China's Social Development; Analysis and Forecast [English Translation].* Leiden: Brill, pp. 245–262.

Zhang Houyi (2007) "Xin Shiji Xin Jieduan de Zhongguo Siying Qiye Zhu Jieceng [A New Century and a New Stage for China's Private Entrepreneurs]," in Ru Xin, Lu Xueyi and Li Peilin (eds.) *2007 Nian: Zhongguo Shehui Xingshi Fenxi yu yu ce* [Analysis and Forecast of China's Social Development]. Beijing: Shehui Kexue Wenxian Chubanshe, pp. 304–320.

Zhang Houyi (2008) "Zhongguo Siying Qiye Zhu Jieceng: Chengzhang Guocheng Zhong de Zhengzhi Canyu [China's Private Entrepreneurial Class: Political Participation in the Course of Growth]," in Ru Xin, Lu Xueyi and Li Peilin (eds.) *2008 Nian: Zhongguo Shehui Xingshi Fenxi yu yu ce* [Analysis and Forecast of China's Social Development]. Beijing: Shehui Kexue Wenxian Chubanshe.

Zhang Houyi (2009) "Zhongguo Siyingqiye Zhu Jieceng ChengZhang de Xin Jieduan, Qingkuang, Xin Wenti [New Phase, Circumstances, and Issues Regarding the Growth of China's Private Entrepreneurial Class]," in Ru Xin, Lu Xueyi and Li Peilin (eds.) *2009 Nian: Zhongguo Shehui Xingshi Fenxi yu yu ce* [Analysis and Forecast of China's Social Development]. Beijing: Shehui Kexue Wenxian Chubanshe, pp. 344–357.

Zhang Houyi (2011) "Siying Qiye Zhu Jieceng Chengzhang Guocheng Zhong de Wenti Ruogan Fenxi [Some Questions and Analysis on the Growth of China's Private Entrepreneurs]," in Ru Xin, Lu Xueyi and Li Peilin (eds.) *2011 Nian: Zhongguo Shehui Xingshi Fenxi yu yu ce* [Analysis and Forecast of China's Social Development]. Beijing: Shehui Kexue Wenxian Chubanshe, pp. 273–285.

Zhang Houyi and Chen Guangjin (2002) "Dangyuan Siying Qiye Zhu Wenjuan Diaocha Fenxi Baogao" [Analytic Report on Survey Data of Private Entrepreneurs who are Party Members], in Zhang Houyi, Ming Lizhi, and Liang Zhuanyuan (eds.)

Zhongguo Siying Qiye Fazhan Baogao [Report on the Development of China's Private Enterprises]. Beijing: Shehui Kexue Wenxian Chubanshe, pp. 86–112.

Zhang Houyi and Liu Pingqing (2004) "Siqi Canzheng' [Private Entrepreneurs' Political Participation]," *Zhujiang Jingji,* 1: pp. 59–61.

Zhang Houyi and Liu Pingqing (2004b) "Siying Qiye Zhu Jieceng Zhong de Gongchandangyuan [Chinese Communist Party Members Among the Private Entrepreneurial Class]," *Chengshi Ban,* 1: pp. 47–48.

Zhongguo Jingji Shibao (2013) "Qiyejia Qiwang Jiakuai Shichanghua Gaige" [Entrepreneurs Hope for Accelerated Marketization Reforms], 05 November. Available at: www.apabi.com

Zhongguo Jingji Shibao (2014) "Yong Fazhi Huhang, Bie Rang Minyingqiyejia 'Zhengde Yue Duoxin Yue Huang' " [Use the Rule of Law to Protect, Don't Make Private Entrepreneurs Feel that "Earning Leads to Worry and Uncertainty"], 27 March. Available at: www.apabi.com.

Zhu Huaxin, Shan Xuegang, and Hu Jiangchun (ZSH) (2011) "Analysis Report on Internet Public Opinion in China in 2008," in Ru Xin, Lu Xueyi, and Li Peilin (eds.) *The China Society Yearbook, Volume 4 [Translated from the Chinese edition: 2009 Nian: Zhongguo Shehui Xingshi Fenxi yu Yuce].* Leiden: Brill, pp. 303–331.

Index

About the Author

Michael Drake has worked in the federal sector since 2018 and has closely studied China's political history for nearly fifteen years. He has conducted extensive field research in China, taught academic courses on Chinese politics and Chinese history, and continues to follow China's contemporary politics and foreign relations.